MUSIC IN OUR LIVES:
the early years

About the Author

Dorothy McDonald is professor emeritus of music education
at the University of Iowa, Iowa City, Iowa. She has taught music from preschool through the university level and has a special interest in preschool music. She has coauthored a music
textbook for early childhood music education and has presented
numerous workshops and clinics throughout the country for
early childhood and primary teachers and music educators.

MUSIC IN OUR LIVES:
the early years

Dorothy T. McDonald

National Association for the Education of Young Children
Washington, D.C.

National Association for the Education of Young Children
1509 16th Street, NW
Washington, DC 20036-1426
202-232-8777 or 800-424-2460
www.naeyc.org

Through its publications program the National for the Education for the Young Children (NAEYC) provides a forum for discussion of major issues and ideas in the early childhood field,
with the hope of provoking thought and promoting professional
growth. The views expressed or implied are not necessarily
those of the Association. NAEYC thanks the author, who do-
nated much time and effort to develop this book as a contribu-
tion to the profession.

Library of Congress Catalog Card Number: 79-51509
ISBN 0-912674-65-2
NAEYC #107

Photo credits:
Sally Gale, © 1979, 3
Ellen Levine Ebert, © 1986, 5; © 1979, 10
Candi Logue, © 1979, 12
Jeffrey High, © 1993, 13
Rich Rosenkoetter, © 1979, 17
Subjects & Predicates, © 1993, 21
Sandy Felsenthal, © 1979, 23
Steve Herzog, © 1986, 25
Gerald Marella, © 1993, 26
Elaine M. Ward, © 1979, 30, 47
Marietta Lynch, © 1993, 33, 40
Diane Wasserman, © 1986, 39
BmPorter/Don Franklin, © 1993, 42

Cover design: Sandi Collins
Music notation: Caroline Taylor

Printed in the United States of America

Contents

Preface

The value of anything we learn in school lies in the extent to which it helps us to respond to the world around us. . . . (Paynter and Aston 1970, p. 2)

This book is about children, teachers, and their music in early childhood programs. It has been prepared to bring together information, from experience and research, about the musical behaviors of young children so teachers may plan musical experiences that are appropriate, meaningful, and enjoyable for both children and teachers. The rapid growth of early childhood programs during the last decade and the recent research evidence that cognitive development is affected by early childhood experiences (Dowley 1969) have produced increased interest in all aspects of children's learning potential. Music educators are especially aware of the need to emphasize meaningful early childhood musical experiences. Before formulating objectives, specifying techniques, or selecting materials for these experiences, we must first understand the musical development of young children. This book has been prepared to provide background for understanding the musical development of children from infancy through age five or six.

Acknowledgment

This book is the result of the combined research efforts and experience of me and my invaluable assistant, Jonny Ramsey, who, while completing her graduate work at the University of Iowa, cooperated with me in identifying existing research reports, compiling and synthesizing information, and conducting experimental studies with young children. Mrs. Ramsey is currently an assistant coordinator in The Pennsylvania Arts in Elementary Education Project, Philipsburg, Pennsylvania, an Elementary and Secondary Education Act Title IV, Part C, cooperative effort between the Central Intermediate Unit #10 and the Fine Arts Program of the Pennsylvania Department of Education.

Dorothy T. McDonald
May 1979

1

The Significance of Music for Learning

Music education for young children is generally dependent upon parents, teachers, and other adults in their lives. Music specialists seldom have been involved in planning or teaching music in early childhood programs. Their contact with children may not begin until after the first two or three years in elementary school. In the rather extensive body of literature on child development, references to children's musical development are rare. Music has generally been accepted as a pleasant addition to an early childhood curriculum, but perhaps not all that important.

Yet, when one considers the prevalence of music in the lives of most young children, this seems curious. Of all age groups, these children probably are our most persistent music makers. They create more music, explore music more conscientiously, use music more consistently and spontaneously, and are more strongly motivated toward music than any other age group. Anyone observing young children at play, at rest, or engaged in any learning activity will not have to wait long before music and rhythm, consciously created by the children, are heard.

Kathy, age three, seemed particularly motivated to song making whenever she was in the swing on the playground. Her spontaneous songs were interesting to listen to. Many were free improvisations built from a snatch of a known song or a single word. Others were wordless melodies, always returning to a single tone. Many could be described as scale songs, moving up and down as she matched the motion of the swing.

No one had told Kathy how her songs should go. The motion of the swing, and her happy feelings, inspired them.

Amelia, a mature four-year-old, arrived at the center one morning with the exciting news that she had a new baby brother. After the general announcement, she went to the instrument shelf, took down a drum, and started beating a rhythm pattern that had come to be identified with her rhythmic play because of her frequent use of it (♩♩♩♫|♩♩♩♪). She said to the children around her, "Let's have a parade!" And so they did, enjoying the activity for a short time, then gradually leaving for other activities.

Amelia's parade cadence was motivated by heightened emotion. Music seemed a natural way of expressing it. She used her own favorite rhythm pattern, which had been refined through repetition.

Bobby, age two and a half, became very interested in the sound he produced one day, quite by accident, when he hit two blocks of wood together in the block-building area.

Forgetting his building project for a time, he concentrated on hitting the blocks in a steady, unaccented-beat pattern. He then hit the blocks on the floor, producing a different sound, and spent a short time trying out various combinations of the two sounds.

Bobby was exploring timbre, or tone color, which has been called the "deepest interest of young children" (Moorhead and Pond 1942, p. 17).

None of these musical happenings was unusual, unique in nature to these children, or particularly extraordinary. Observational records of most children contain similar descriptions of such music making.

Perhaps the best known of such records of young children's musical activities are those produced by the Pillsbury Foundation. In 1937, this foundation launched an in-depth study of the spontaneous music activities of young children two to six years old. Many insights about the kinds of music young children create individually and with other children are detailed in the reports of the study. After observing the musical behaviors of young children over a period of several years, the authors described music as:

> . . . not an isolated thing, it is part of a life-process; it is separate neither from the child's consciousness nor from any aspect of . . . everyday life. . . . For the child . . . lives, and makes music. Music, for the child, is something; it exists for his life's sake; it is an inner expression on behalf of himself as a personality and as a member of a society. (Moorhead and Pond 1942, pp. 20-21)

Whether or not teachers of young children include music in their daily activities, it is there because children bring with them their ability to make and respond to music.

The development of musical skills and understandings that can enhance children's natural enjoyment of music is dependent upon the leadership of teachers and others who have learned how children use music, have discovered the abilities a particular group of children have in specific areas of music, and, using such information, have formulated appropriate goals and objectives. Music learning cannot happen entirely spontaneously. The set of song bells left on the table of the music interest center, never used by an adult in a musical way, falls into disuse. The record receiving no more attention from an adult than its placement on the turntable, produces only audible wallpaper.

Music may be present in an early childhood center because children are there, but its significance for learning often depends upon the teacher who plans for its presence. Children show us how and where to begin through their spontaneous music making; adults are necessary to plan where to go and how to get there. What goals and objectives are reasonable and appropriate? And when should music experiences begin?

When should planned musical experiences begin?

Attention to musical sound, and interest in producing musical sounds, begins in infancy. Several studies have noted the focused attention given to music by infants in their first six months, their attempts to carry on "musical conversations"

Music may be present in an early childhood center because children are there, but its significance for learning often depends upon the teacher who plans for its presence.

with others before the age of one year, and their rhythmic and dancelike movements when music is present. Two researchers suggest that:

> Children use music as a form of
> expression very early in their
> development. It is said that the child can
> sing before he talks, and some attempt at
> expression through music may be
> observed in practically all children.
> (Merry and Merry 1950, p. 557)

In view of these findings, the starting time for learning about music is the same as the starting time for any learning. Music is one facet in the total education of the child. It must emerge with the nature and needs of the child, from birth onward.

Viewed in this context, planned musical experiences should not be withheld until children are old enough to join in group singing activities or until they are able to keep time in rhythmic games. Music learning is going on long before the traditional group music activities of school.

What are reasonable goals and objectives?

Musical skills compatible with the ages of young children (two to six years old) and their developmental stages of learning (sensorimotor and preoperational) might include the following:

1. Learning to sing tunefully.
2. Learning to respond rhythmically to music through creative movement and instrumental expression.
3. Learning to play simple classroom instruments that do not require fine muscular coordination.

4. Learning to develop attentive listening habits.
(Zimmerman 1975, p. 20)

These musical skills, nurtured, extended, refined, and developed as the child grows, might serve as reasonable objectives for an early childhood music curriculum. Zimmerman has also suggested that withholding the kinds of experiences that could develop certain musical skills and understandings during critical stages of maturation and development can cause those skills to remain undeveloped. The early childhood years are increasingly being recognized as critical years for many aspects of musical growth.

Providing for curriculum activities

A music curriculum for any early childhood program that could provide a firm foundation for the development of the kinds of skills (and concomitant understandings) listed above involves interaction among children, teachers, and music. Children's musical development is dependent upon their active involvement in the process of making music. They have feelings for the music they create, but because many of these feelings are nonverbal and sensory in character, they need adults to assist them in awakening their awareness of what their singing voices can do, what their bodies can express rhythmically, and what their hands and fingers can produce on musical instruments. Moreover, they need adults to help them become acquainted with many kinds of music.

The children. Children in any group bring a wide variety of musical abilities and experiences as a result of their other experiences and maturation. These differences are probably greatest during the first five years of life.

April was three years old and an extremely verbal child. She loved to join in group singing, and her singing accompanied most of her individual activities. Her repertoire of learned songs was extensive, but she improvised and created songs easily and often as well. She sang accurately and tunefully, using a wide pitch range. Her mother often sang with her at home, and singing was a natural form of expression for April. She explained to the teacher, "We don't got a piano; Mommy sings with me!"

One of April's friends was Aaron, who was two months older.

Aaron had had little experience with singing. He seldom joined the group for singing. Instead, he chose to watch and listen from a distant, "safe" vantage point. Occasionally he would join in a favorite song, usually only whispering the words.

Among the younger group was Becky, age two and a half.

Becky regarded group singing as a fine time for joining the other children socially, but not to sing! She listened attentively, however, and observed the teacher and the other children with interest. Later she was often heard singing snatches of these songs to herself.

One of the most enthusiastic singers was four-year-old Curt. An energetic, outgoing youngster, Curt joined lustily and joyfully in group singing, seldom in tune, but always with great satisfaction.

If the first of our listed objectives—learning to sing tunefully—is to be realized by all of these children, it is necessary to take into consideration their different stages of development of this skill, and proceed from there. Aaron needs

time and experience to formulate his concept of what singing is. He needs to gain voco-motor control through many opportunities to explore and experiment with singing and melody making. Becky is assimilating the sounds and ways of singing. For Curt, accurate singing is a not-too-distant goal to be achieved when voco-motor control, experience, and maturation come together and match his motivation! April helps her

We must be willing to listen to what the children are doing, observe their musical responses, learn to build musical experiences from these, and desire to bring music to children.

5

friends by providing a model of accurate singing and enjoyment in the skill. Whatever their stage of development, all these children may possess excellent musical potential.

Such individual differences also exist in rhythmic, instrumental, and listening skills. Therefore, it is important that a sense of developmental stages, dependent upon many factors besides age, be considered. The sequential development of these musical skills, with suggestions to teachers for implementing experiences that help reach appropriate goals, are further explored in Chapter 2. Piaget has reminded us, "The ideal of education is not to teach the maximum . . . but to learn to learn, to learn to develop, and to learn to continue to develop" (Zimmerman 1975, p. 14).

The teacher. As in all other areas, only by starting where the children are musically can a music curriculum make sense. Teachers first need to recognize what children are doing musically in their spontaneous music-making activities. Taking cues from the children, we may encourage, extend, and help develop children's skills through an organized plan rather than trusting that a variety of activities and songs will accomplish our goals. However, an organized approach to early music curriculum experiences does not necessarily mean a planned, regularly scheduled music period each day. Teachers of young children find that if they listen and observe, teachable moments occur at any time of the day.

For example, three-and-a-half-year-old James, experimenting with a set of tone bells, announced that the bar to the left was "very tall and high like Daddy"; further, the small one was the "baby" (the one farthest to the right) and very "low." James was verbalizing a common, almost classic confusion about musical pitch. James was using the size of himself and his father ("low" and "high") to compare and describe relative musical pitches. His logic, understandable and reasonable, resulted in a completely turned around definition of "high" and "low" when applied to musical pitch. Instead of laughing and correcting him, we took time to discuss another way of viewing this idea—"Daddy's *voice* is low; and that describes the longer tone bar, also." James brought up this alternative idea on a number of successive days, almost reciting each time the new way of thinking about "high" and "low" on the tone bars while he played them. He gradually seemed to accept this way of thinking about the verbal descriptors.

Many such opportunities for impromptu teaching will occur. As teachers or parents of young children, however, we must realize it is also of utmost importance that we take time not only to teach about music but also to approve and appreciate the children's spontaneously created music. We should remember that we provide models for children—adults who value music as part of daily life, or adults who do not value it. These values are sensed by the children. Being models may be our most important responsibility.

Perhaps one of the reasons music is neglected in early childhood is that many teachers have regarded it as a group experience, almost wholly teacher-directed and teacher-initiated. But this is not the way that young children typically use music. They do not wait for "music time" to sing, compose, dance, listen. Although some group experiences are desirable (and have value in building social skills and increasing musical exchanges among children), many younger children find it difficult to tolerate large-group activities for more than a very short time. It is best, therefore, not to confine music to a planned, rigidly scheduled music period. Rather, music should be encouraged and incorporated as a specific part of many daily activities, including science, language, and movement exploration.

Musical abilities of the early childhood teacher need not be extensive. Can you sing the traditional songs and folk tunes that have always been loved by children? Children are not critics. They enjoy singing with an adult who loves and appreciates music. Can you create and improvise simple rhymes and chants about daily occurrences and activities? Young children enjoy personalized musical experiences. Can you, when observing a child producing a rhythmic sound, "pick up" the child's rhythm on a drum, triangle, or piano? Can you bring favorite musical recordings to share with the children? Teacher appreciation and approval have been cited in research as significant factors in children's willingness to listen to unfamiliar music (Greer, Dorow, and Hanser 1973). We must be willing to *listen* to what the children are doing, *observe* their musical responses, *learn* to build musical experiences from these, and *desire* to bring music to children.

The music. What kinds of music are most appropriate for use in an early childhood music curriculum? The best music to begin with is that of the child's immediate environment.

In one center was Jennie, who came from a family whose church played an important role in their lives. Jennie loved the strongly rhythmic folk hymns and gospel songs she had learned in church, and many of her spontaneous play tunes reflected these melodies. Annette's older sister studied ballet, and Annette found special delight in creating sweeping dance movements for selections from Tchaikovsky's *Sleeping Beauty* ballet. Rodney's favorite was the "Sesame Street" theme song. Laura found special satisfaction in experimenting with tone bars and was able accurately to play a number of the nursery songs she knew—"Twinkle, Twinkle, Little Star" was her latest accomplishment. Bobby was most excited when a visiting parent brought a guitar to the center and sang Mexican-American

folksongs for the children. He would sit very near the performer, and would often rest his hand on the guitar as it was being played. A Folkways recording of Javanese gamelon instrumental music was enjoyed by many of the children.

Gospel, classical, contemporary popular, nursery songs, folk music—they all belong. Should we rely on a single type of music for young children? Not if we take our cues from the children.

In addition to providing experiences with many kinds of serious, contemporary popular, folk, and ethnic music, however, we must enlarge the traditional definition of *music*. Music for young children is, first of all, sound that is used for self-expression. Children are natural explorers of sound and creators of music. The products of this exploration are rightfully part of a music curriculum. With this enlarged definition of music, infants' crylike sounds have been described as "ancestors of soft melodic sounds composed of gliding tones" (Moorhead and Pond 1942, p. 12).

As children grow, they produce experimental, spontaneous songs, using melody in interesting and unique ways, not necessarily in the ways of the more traditional and familiar songs usually taught. As children develop language skills, word patterns often turn into songs, and rhythmic speech often becomes vocal chant. Exploratory experiences with instruments often produce unusual compositions, combining interesting instrumental timbres and rhythms.

\#   \#   \#

Children's musical behaviors from infancy through age five or six, the role of the teacher in planning musical experiences, and some of the music created or chosen by children follow in this book. This information is intended to help adults understand what children are doing musically and may aid in planning appropriate musical experiences. Through music the child's imagination, feeling of self-worth, and capacity for self-expression can be nurtured and given room for growth.

> Music for the young child starts with
> **exploration, imitation, experimentation**
> which can lead to
> **discrimination, organization, creation**
> which, in turn, can lead to
> **reorganization, production, conceptualization.**

References and suggested readings

Dowley, E. "Early Childhood Education." In *Encyclopedia of Educational Research*, ed. R. L. Ebel. 4th ed. London: Macmillian Co., 1969.

Greer, R. D.; Dorow. L.; and Hanser, S. "Music Discrimination Training and the Music Selection Behavior of Nursery and Primary Level Children." *Council for Research in Music Education Bulletin* 35 (Winter 1973): 30-43.

Merry, F. F., and Merry, R. V. *The First Two Decades of Life.* New York: Harper and Brothers, 1950.

Moorhead, G. E., and Pond, D. *Music of Young Children, II. General Observations.* Santa Barbara, Calif.: Pillsbury Foundation for Advancement of Music Education, November 1942.

Paynter, J., and Aston, P. *Sound and Silence.* Cambridge, England: University Press, 1970.

Zimmerman, M. P. "Research in Music Education with Very Young Children." *Music Education for the Very Young Child (Report of the Fourth International Seminar on Research in Music Education).* Wellington, New Zealand: New Zealand Council for Educational Research, 1975.

2

Children: The Development of Musical Skills

At no time in the life of a child is the world so full of promise as in the first five or six years, for during no other period do children accomplish so much. At two years old, many children are just beginning to talk; they verbalize single words but few whole sentences. They walk, but fall easily when turning quickly or when running. They live in the "here and now," having little concept of past or future. They often do not play successfully with other children, having limited understanding of sharing or cooperation. They want to do things their way. Social relationships are awkward. They need adults to care for their physical and emotional needs.

Contrast this with a five-year-old. By five, children have developed individual personalities. Their special skills and abilities are becoming identifiable. They have an extensive vocabulary and enjoy carrying on conversations with other children. They play easily with other children and want to be with them. They run, skip, gallop. They make up rhymes, poems, chants, songs, and stories.

Such pronounced physical, verbal, and social changes take place gradually during this four-year period. They result from interactions among homes, schools, and communities that foster healthful growth and provide guidance from caring parents, teachers, and other people involved in the child's life.

Similarly, growth in musical skills and understanding is a

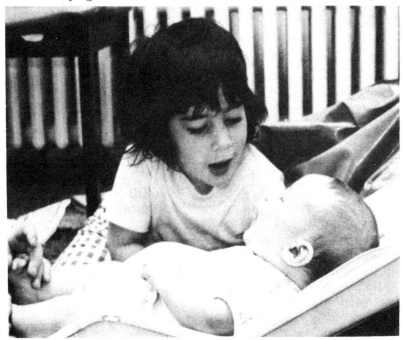

"Musical" children are usually found in abundance in environments where music is valued, explored, and included in daily living. The development of a "musical" child begins in infancy.

gradual process resulting from environmental and personal influences. Too often, musical skills are erroneously regarded as inborn and inherited. If children are able to sing tunefully at age three, or if they are responsive to rhythm at even younger ages, we often feel that these are the "musical" children. While individual differences among children are as great in musical skills as in any other kind of skill or ability, "musical" children are usually found in abundance in environments where music is valued, explored, and included in daily living. And the development of a "musical" child begins in infancy.

Infants as musicians

Rarely do we consider an infant capable of exhibiting musical behaviors. Sing? Move rhythmically to music? Listen to music attentively? Infants *do*, according to studies of very young children. Because music exists as a form of aural communication, it is used by all people and by people of all ages. Even an infant, first as a "receiver," and gradually as a "participant," uses music as a preverbal way of communicating with the outside world. Noy (1968) described music as an "auditory channel"—one of the preverbal ways children receive signals in the first months of life before their egos can distinctly delineate the boundaries between self and reality. This researcher felt that if music was a primary mode of communication between mother and infant, it would continue to be important in the child's emotional exchange with the world.

Infants are attentive to musical sounds in their environment and they soon begin to sort them out from other sounds. An interesting account of this early attention to music has been reported by Michel who wrote that "at two months, an infant will lie motionless, with fixed attention if anyone sings or plays an instrument," and that ". . . at five months this attention may last for half an hour'' (1973, p. 15). McDonald has suggested that some young children may identify and use a certain tune associated with a home shared or comforting experience as a transitional object, just as some use a favorite toy or familiar blanket to help master separation and aloneness and make acquaintance with the outside world more pleasurable (1970).

As the process of sorting out sounds from an environment full of aural stimuli progresses, infants begin to discriminate their own vocal sounds from those of others, and use them to communicate with other persons. At very early ages, they appear to try to imitate what they hear. Ostwald (1973) called this period one of *vocal contagion*—the period when babies become interested in environmental sounds to the extent that they are stimulated to participate. This period may begin before the second half of the first year. Such vocalizations have been called *laling* and *trilling* and have been studied for their melodic characteristics and for the situations that evoked them. In some cultures nurses of very young children are specifically instructed to encourage these infant-songs by mimicking them (Ostwald 1973). Imitation of sounds is enjoyed by babies; many will spend long periods in such vocal play.

Infants' musical behaviors are not limited to vocal imitation or attentive listening. At about the age of six months, children may begin to respond to music by overt movement—" . . . not in an unorganized, clumsy way, but with very clear repetitive movements'' (Moog 1976, p. 39) using whole body movements in preference to individual parts. Although these responses may not be in synchronization with the rhythmic stimulus, or participatory, they should be recognized as musical responses. Zimmerman also found that before the age of one year, " . . . body and facial responses to orchestral and choral music occurred more readily among one- to eleven-month-olds than did participatory and imitative responses'' (1975, p. 13).

We cannot dismiss even the first year of a child's life as one in which nothing happens musically. From receiver to participator. From participator to creator. From listening to sound to making sound to making music.

What can adults in nursery schools, infant-care centers, or at home do to nurture the attention and response that infants instinctively give to music? Because first attention is to discrimination of pitch and timbre, we should provide many experiences with sounds of different pitches and timbres—musical and otherwise—for infants. Crib mobiles make interesting sounds when the baby bats them or the wind moves them. Rattles, which have been described as the child's first instrument, made from various materials provide similar sound stimulation experiences (Voglar 1977). Music boxes provide interesting contrasts in timbre and pitch. Caregiving tasks provide adults with many opportunities for rhythmic and melodic musical exchanges. Are lullabies sung to children? One teenager still feels "special," she says, when she hears "The Riddle Song," the lullaby her mother sang to her, although she cannot remember the actual experience. "Pat-a-cake," "Peek-a-boo," "This Little Piggie"—games like these as well as nursery rhymes and songs can delight the infant and encourage attentive listening and sometimes delightful participation. Spontaneously created rhymes, chanted or sung, are enjoyed. Recordings of music, not played constantly as background music, but at selected times, give obvious pleasure to infants. Especially prepared for infants' listening are two recent albums, *Music for the Morning of Life* (Arrive Recording Studios) and *Loving and Learning from Birth to Three* (Joy Records). Providing an environment in which music is valued enhances daily routines, and is enjoyed by adults as well as the very young children—the first step in developing musical interest and awareness in young children.

Although the first year of life may be regarded as a musical *receiving* year, it is evident that musical responsiveness begins here. Between the ages of two and six, however, an astounding amount of musical growth takes place. One can hardly lump these years together in a discussion of musical behaviors, as the two-year-old and six-year-old are quite different in musical responses and abilities. For this reason, let us first look at very young children from about age two to three and a half or four.

Very young children

When children reach two years of age, most have learned to walk and talk, the most important developments in their lives up to this time. These skills have much influence on their musical development, and music generally elicits alert, active responses from these children. Although their attention span is brief, and their interest in participating in group activities is limited, they are quite persistent music makers. They enjoy singing, both spontaneously and imitatively. They explore and experiment with rhythmic movement. They show great interest in the sound characteristic of musical instruments and all sound-producing objects. They may show concentrated, attentive attitudes when listening to music. They assimilate a great repertoire of sounds and movements; the nature and extent of their musical responsiveness grows and expands. Music seems a natural form of expression. Given freedom and opportunity, they are natural explorers of sound.

Often, however, music making is an individual activity. Very young children make little attempt to organize their music

Music making is often an individual activity for very young children.

making into group activities, except when, by accident, such situations occur. We may observe Daudi pushing a fire truck, singing "ding-dong" (a descending melodic fourth) as he moves it around the floor. Paige, only a few feet away, is climbing up the climbing bars, and is matching her climb with an improvised ascending melody, fitting it with words, "Climbing up the stairs." Loren, lying on the floor by himself, sings, "Ho, hum; I got a cow. Don't you know, a big brown cow." The tune revolves around a single tone. Jeff and Rhashetta, who have been playing together, suddenly break into spontaneous duet—"I do! I do! I do!"—which covers quite a wide pitch range of descending minor thirds. The duet ends in giggling and laughter. Lara listens to a record, headphones in place, and hums as she listens. Esteban makes tentative experimental sounds on a drum that he has chosen from the instrument shelf, and is joined by Amelia, who accompanies his drum beat with her favorite rhythm pattern on the tambourine.

Studies of the spontaneous musical activities of children like these provide information about *what* they are doing with singing and rhythm. Let us consider singing skills first.

Learning to sing

Studies of very young children's singing activities include those of Simons (1964), Alford (1971), Young (1971), and Smith (1963). Findings from these studies provide the following information about beginning singing skills:

♪ By age two, most children sing as we generally recognize the skill. Much of their singing is self-generated and spontaneous, occurring as individual exploratory experiences with melody or playing with language.

♪ The pitch range of their spontaneous singing can be quite extensive. From A♭ below middle C to the C♯ an octave above middle C has been reported. However, when learning songs by imitation, a limited range of from D to A (above middle C) seems to be their most comfortable, usable range.

♪ Many spontaneous songs grow out of motor activities or play with language and vocabulary, and language development may be enhanced by creating simple songs containing repetitive words or phrases.

♪ Their spontaneous songs frequently use the "teasing chant" melodic configuration (as in "Rain, Rain, Go

The process of learning to sing tunefully depends upon opportunities and encouragement to explore, experiment, and manipulate vocal sound. Many young children regard group singing experiences as opportunities to listen without joining in.

Away"). Songs with large melodic intervals are more difficult to sing than those with smaller ones. When melodies contain intervals larger than a fifth or sixth, young children often compress them so that they fit into their easily used pitch range.

♪ Very young children are not attentive to the necessity to match pitch or tonality when singing with others. Rather, they choose their own pitch range. You may match your pitch to those of the children and in this way introduce the concept of singing in unison.

♪ Two- and three-year-old children often sing only snatches of songs. Between the ages of two and three there is considerable progress in the ability to reproduce songs in their entirety. Many three-year-olds are able to sing whole songs accurately and develop a large repertoire of songs.

♪ Many young children regard group singing experiences as opportunities to listen without joining in. When they do sing, they often lag behind a bit. Sometimes they begin participating by whispering the words. Often they sing only parts of songs—perhaps a repeated phrase that has caught their attention. They enjoy listening to favorite songs over and over and need many opportunities to listen before they become participants in group singing.

The process of learning to sing tunefully depends upon opportunities (and encouragement) to explore, experiment, and manipulate vocal sound. Learning to sing takes place gradually and inevitably (given an environment that allows its growth) and is inseparable from other growth processes.

To learn to sing, children must know what it feels like to sing and how it sounds to match pitches with others. Children need positive feedback so they know when they are matching pitches

and thus can formulate a model for themselves. They must have opportunities to talk and sing individually, to learn to control high and low in vocal speech and song (Shelley 1976, p. 211). A developmental description of the process of learning to sing has been provided in studies by Young (1971a) and Smith (1963). In the initial stage, young children attempt to use the range of their speaking voices to sing. They often focus upon one prominent feature of a song, perhaps a repeated melodic or rhythmic phrase. Song singing at this stage has been described as ". . . monotonous singing in a comfortable tone or rhythmic range because it reproduces only the rhythmic curve of a melody" (Ilina 1960, p. 108).

What does research concerning the development of singing ability suggest to teachers? First of all, we should remember that learning to sing follows stages that are not necessarily related to age. Songs chosen for very young children should include those of limited range, perhaps five or six tones, with melodic intervals that are easy for children to reproduce. Many familiar folksongs fit these criteria—"Go Tell Aunt Rhody," "This Old Man," "Twinkle, Twinkle, Little Star," and many others. Most of the songs should lie in the pitch range from approximately middle C to the A above.

Although quite complex contemporary children's songs heard on TV, radio, and recordings are attractive to children, many of them are more easily listened to than sung by very young children. However, we should include songs that are fun to listen to as well as those that are easily sung! The teacher must have realistic expectations about which will be most accurately reproduced. Children should be allowed at times to pitch songs themselves, choosing their own comfortable singing ranges. The teacher may then match the children's pitch; children may develop a perceptual awareness of pitch matching, a necessary skill for successful group singing.

Following this stage, teachers might become aware of directional singing. Although the vocal ranges of the children have expanded, many seem unable to use their expanded ranges to duplicate the direction of a melody accurately. They may move up or down, but not necessarily in the direction of the melody. As directional singing becomes more accurate, reproduction of melodic intervals may still remain inexact.

Experience and maturation enable young singers to reproduce accurately pitch and melodic interval. We may find children whose perception of melodic intervals exceeds the physical capabilities of their voices; often these children are able accurately to reproduce a lower, transposed version of the melody (Young 1971b).

Exploring rhythm

Music and rhythmic movement are closely related for young children. Awareness of various aspects of music is often first expressed through movement. Studies of the spontaneous singing of children have shown that song itself often grows out of motor rhythm and first attention to taught songs is upon the rhythmic aspects. Greenberg (1972) reported that concepts of beat, tempo, and dynamics develop first in young children while those of pitch and melody, melodic rhythm, harmony, and form develop at a much slower pace.

Learning to move rhythmically, and to be able to control rhythmic responses to music, has been described by Moog as ". . . a most important step forward in children's cognitive development" (1976, p. 41). Children who acquire good motor skills and who are able to find their own body rhythms are able to express what they perceive. Too often, however, the requirement to keep time to music in various ways is imposed upon young children who often are not able to do this. Beginning rhythmic experiences should encourage children to enjoy moving rhythmically in their own ways—to *explore* rhythmic movement.

Tony (age two years, eight months) was an uncommunicative child, who had limited language skills. Clumping about in the heavy cowboy boots he wore to school every day, he seldom participated in any group activities except rarely as a short-term observer. He never joined in rhythmic activities. One day the teacher put on a recording of a march. Tony, becoming aware of the strongly rhythmic music, stopped what he was doing and began to bend his knees, moving up and down ever so slightly. Pleased with this, he smiled and began moving his arms from side to side, also. The teacher observed, "Tony, your legs and arms are marching to the music!" Tony's march became more emphatic; the satisfaction he felt was reflected in his broad smile. Seldom did he "synchronize" with the beat of the music; instead he was exploring the possibilities of matching this kind of movement with that kind of music.

Findings from studies by Christianson (1938), Scheihing (1951), Moorhead and Pond (Shuter 1968), Simons (1964), and Jersild and Bienstock (1935) about the spontaneous and imitative rhythmic responses of two- and three-year-old children seem to indicate that:

- Two-year-old children tend to respond actively to markedly rhythmic music, but each at his or her own tempo.
- The body rhythms of very young children often are at faster tempi than those that might seem comfortable for adults.
- Synchronization with music may occur only when it is well adapted to the child's rate of movement. Drill on keeping time does not seem to improve the skill.

♪Children two and three years old often keep to one type of movement throughout a rhythmic experience; repetition helps them develop perceptual understanding of the relationship between music pulse and movement.

♪By age three, many children have acquired some ability in synchronizing movement with rhythmic stimuli for a limited period of time.

♪With greater motor coordination and increasing ability to control rhythmic responses, three-year-old children are more likely to experiment with use of space and a variety of body movements in their responses.

For young children, the beginnings of understanding rhythmic concepts about music lie in movement and their abilities to match movement with music. Keeping time with music, however, is a skill that is gradually developed. Teachers should emphasize exploratory experiences with rhythm using recordings and songs that invite gross responses rather than synchronization. Acquiring a repertoire of rhythmic movements (through exploratory and imitative activities) is important and comes from many experiences, including nonmusical ones. Rhyming or chanting, for example, can serve as stimuli.

If, in rhythmic play, a uniform tempo is established by the children, you may improvise word rhythms that fit the children's movements or accompany them with drum, tambourine, or hand clapping. Similarly, the rhythm of a child's walk, skip, or run may be matched. Meanings of fast and slow, even and uneven, may then be discussed. Action songs ("Ring Around the Rosy," "The Hokey Pokey") and fingerplay songs ("The Rabbit in the Wood," "The Wheels on the Bus") offer opportunities for rhythmic movement without the requirement of beat synchronization. Following the suggestions given for an activity to accompany "Old Joe Clarke," in Seeger's *American Folk Songs for Children*, one group of four-year-old children explored countless ways to move "round and round" to fit the words of the song. In short, two- and three-year-olds need opportunities to acquire a repertoire of movements that they may use in creative ways in these early years, rather than drill in keeping time.

Interest in playing instruments

Authentic musical instruments are of great interest to young children. Children should be allowed to use the instruments freely, and teacher direction should be given only when sought. Moorhead, Sandvik, and Wight wrote:

> When simple instruments are presented to young children, they are used as naturally as blocks or paints. . . . The sounds that (the child) hears and the sounds that he makes with the materials around him become also a part of his musical experience. By the use of simple musical instruments he extends his experience in tone and rhythm and develops new forms of expression. (1951, p. 3)

Instruments provide children with experiences in rhythm, melody, and harmony. For young children, however, they are, first of all, something that produces an individual and unique sound. Voglar wrote that " . . . at the age of two, the child satisfies his inclination to produce sounds by finding himself those objects which are sound-producing. Here he is very inventive, making use of everything he gets his hands on: dishes and cutlery, toys, etc." (1977, p. 136). These objects are musical instruments to young children. In one center, a group working with clay made instruments of their clay forms; some beat the forms on the table; some patted their hands on the balls; one child started a chant, "Play dough, play dough." Other children joined in creating an interesting contrapuntal composition.

Similarly, when standard rhythm and melody instruments are introduced, young children do not initially use them to produce rhythms or tunes but to experience sound. Voglar described her young group's first experiences:

> . . . they were simply enraptured by the sounds they produced with these instruments. They did not produce a definite rhythm pattern, but only isolated sounds. . . . Some of them put the instruments to their ears, others would put it against the ear of a friend. . . . In this case, the children were directed solely to sound-producing. (1977, p. 136)

When introducing instruments to young children (one at a time is advised), the children are interested, first of all, in the instrument itself, as well as what it can do. They will want to

---

When standard rhythm and melody instruments are introduced, young children do not initially use them to produce rhythms or tunes but to experience sound.

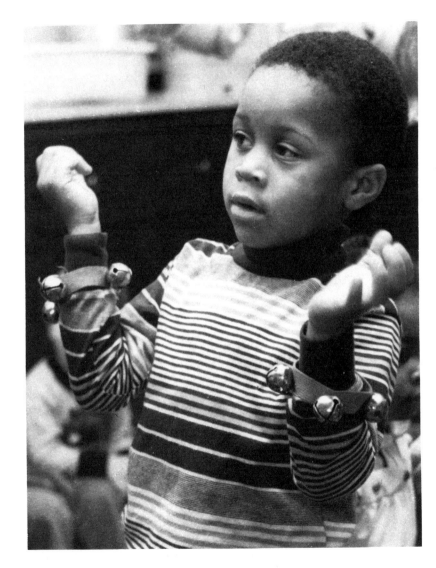

examine it—to feel it and experiment with the ways it can produce sounds. Teachers should encourage this exploration. Can the children identify the instrument by name? Can its shape be described—round, oval, square, triangular? Can its shape be recognized when drawn on chalkboard or paper? Is its sound loud or soft? How can we hold it when we play it so that the sound is most satisfactory? What does its sound remind us of? Parades? Horses? Raindrops? With such an introduction either to individual or groups of children, teachers find that instruments are seldom misused, even by younger children.

An instrument may also be regarded by young children as a new form of an already acquired musical response—possibly a logical substitution for the sounds they have produced with their bodies (fingers, hands, feet). Instruments also may become audible representations of rhythmic movement. The interesting interrelationship between body rhythms and rhythmic expression through instruments has been described by Moorhead and Pond: "He uses instruments while he is moving or after he has been moving; he grows able to abstract his movement rhythms into pure sound" (1942, p. 12). And, " . . . we have seen how instrumental performances by one or a number of children may evoke movement reactions from others who are engaged in other activities" (1942, p. 10).

Instruments for children support movement, suggest it, or represent it, e.g., "Which instrument should we use when we whirl around and around until we fall, like leaves, on the ground? How should we make the sound? Let's let our instruments help us tell the story."

When children first produce rhythmic sounds on instruments, they are in the form of regular, unaccented pulsations (Shuter 1968) that are quite fast in tempo (Scheihing 1951; Simons 1964). If an interesting rhythm pattern is produced, that pattern is often repeated until it is mastered and the child is ready to apply it in different contexts. Thus Amelia's identifiable pattern, described in the first chapter, was heard in many situations and on many different instruments. Little attempt is made by young children to match the rhythms they produce with those of other children; they have an ability to maintain their own rhythm against all others. Training or drill on synchronizing with the beat does not seem to improve this skill significantly; maturation and experience, all through the early years, seem the most important factors in achieving this skill (Jersild and Bienstock 1935, p. 95).

When we provide instruments for very young children, we know that:

♪ Opportunities should be provided to explore the sound-making qualities or timbre of improvised and traditional instruments in free, unstructured situations.

For two- and three-year-old children, instruments should be introduced as natural extensions of the sounds their fingers, hands, and feet can make. Instead of expecting very young children to keep time with instruments to music, you may want to introduce instruments by using them to produce sound effects for stories, poems, chants, or nursery rhymes. In "Hickory Dickory Dock" the clock may strike one, two, or three on a tone bar or triangle at the appropriate time. Sand blocks may be used to imitate a train; triangles make satisfactory water sounds. Rhythm sticks may become ticking clocks; tone bars the call of the cuckoo clock. A cymbal crash may sound like a thunderclap. Drums may accompany parades. When it is appropriate for the children in larger groups to use instruments, such preliminary experiences with individual instruments, introduced gradually, will enable the children to know about the instrument, how it can be used, and how it should be handled and cared for.

♪ Because two- and three-year-olds are interested in all aspects of an instrument, they may be guided in observing, comparing, and talking about its name, appearance, shape, and sound possibilities before any supervised activities using the instrument are introduced.

♪ Very young children should not be expected to keep time to music using instruments, but, rather, should be encouraged to participate in instrumental activities so as to cultivate their interest in and widen their experiences with tone and rhythm.

Selecting instruments. It is difficult to generalize about which instruments elicit greatest interest in exploratory instrumental activities. In one center, during spontaneous play, tambourines and claves were the most popular. Small drums so often inspired spontaneous songs that the teacher kept a tape recorder near the drums so that some of these songs could be recorded for parents and other children to hear. Individual tone bars, two or three at a time, were often placed on the music interest table, and the children enjoyed arranging and rearranging them, exploring the various combinations of the two or three pitches. Mia, age three and a half, produced this song and words with three tone bells after quite a long creative period.

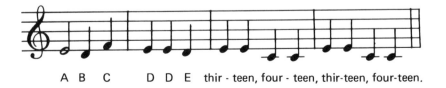

A B C   D D E   thir - teen, four - teen, thir-teen, four-teen.

She sang her song while playing it, matching her pitches with those of the bells. Often, however, vocalizations made by children of these ages are completely unrelated in pitch to the bells or piano notes they choose to accompany the melodies.

Fretted chording instruments such as ukuleles and guitars also interest most young children. The use of these instruments by teachers adds much to singing time because they are portable and can bring the adult closer to the children. Children also enjoy playing these instruments. To produce a satisfactory and easy accompaniment for children to play, teachers may adjust the strings so that a tuned chord results. For example, a baritone ukulele may be tuned (from left to right) to the notes of D, G, B, and D. Children can then strum this chord. Although young children seldom pay attention to fitting their singing to an accompaniment—they " . . . find it more difficult to consider the simultaneous harmonic aspects of a song" (Andress, Heimann, Rinehart, and Calvert 1973, p. 22)—the rhythmic hand movement and the exploratory aspects of producing chords are valuable experiences.

Teachers and adults should become aware of community resources for acquainting young children with musical instruments. Parents or others who play instruments or sing usually are pleased to be invited to share their skills and interests. In one center, it became a special day when the custodian of the building—who always seemed to have his harmonica in his back pocket—dropped by. When he appeared, the children crowded around, and each time he obliged with a performance.

Rhythm instruments may be purchased in sets. Generally these sets may be ordered according to the number of children; for example, a 15-pupil set or 30-pupil set may be ordered. Drums, tambourines, and larger instruments may not be included but may be purchased separately. A rhythm instrument set may include:

Triangles	Claves	Tambourine sticks
Ankle bells	Rhythm sticks	Instructor's book
Wrist bells	Soprano sounder	
Sand blocks	Crow sounder	

Chording instruments, such as autoharps, ukuleles, and guitars, as well as melody instruments, including resonator bells (tone bars), step bells, song bells, and xylophones also are recommended purchases for early childhood programs. A piano is also desirable, and the children should be allowed to use it. There is no better instrument to demonstrate (visually and kinesthetically) what is meant by pitch in music. The piano should be introduced by the teacher in as careful a way as individual classroom instruments are presented.

When instruments are used in musical activities for young children, the process, rather than the product, is the important goal.

> Sounds can be made in a variety of ways on many different objects. Often these sounds can be fascinating and fun to sound and produce. The expressive implications of sounds may vary considerably when they are heard in various sequences and vertical combinations. Children soon learn that they can manipulate and organize the materials of music in ways that infer many different moods and feelings. A new sense of being is discovered; they can create, feel, think, evaluate, reject, interpret, control, express, reason, fashion sounds to their will. (Biasini, Thomas, and Pogonowski 1970, p. 23)

Listening with understanding

Because music is an aural art, the basis of all musical understandings lies in the ability to listen perceptively. Children must listen carefully to learn a song, move appropriately to music, or play an instrument. Their acquaintance with unfamiliar music also is dependent upon their willingness to listen. An important dimension of most early childhood curriculums is the cultivation of auditory perception—listening with understanding:

> A teacher may suggest: "Close your eyes. Listen carefully to all the sounds you hear. Let's talk about them. Where are they coming from? Can you imitate these sounds with your voice?"

Such exercises lead logically to timbre discrimination.

> "From the sound, can you tell which things were hit? Which one did you hear first? And next?" (such as a cymbal, a wood block, a triangle, a tone bar, a drum).

Discriminative listening has been linked to achievement in language and reading; you probably have included many activities of this kind for this reason. However, listening to music for no other reason than to enjoy is an exciting activity in itself. Unfamiliar music can become familiar; musical horizons can be extended.

Introducing new music. Music unfamiliar to children may include records of serious music; music played for the children by visiting performers, parents, or teachers; classical music that is available on TV, radio, films, filmstrips; serious art music; folk music; contemporary composed folk music; and ethnic music. Too often these kinds of music are never included

Chording instruments such as ukuleles, guitars, and autoharps interest most young children.

in early childhood music programs. Perhaps this is because of the short attention spans of very young children. Perhaps this is due to the lack of available guidelines for directing listening activities. Whatever the reason, teachers often feel at a loss to go beyond the contemporary popular recordings with which the children are familiar. Perhaps they may use a recording of a serious composition for background music to accompany a quiet activity. While there is nothing intrinsically wrong with this kind of experience, studies of music listening behaviors of young children indicate that more might be done with this aspect of musical experience.

Studies of infants' responses to musical stimuli suggest that listening attentively to music comes with the child, so to speak. We start out with a listening child. This interest remains as the child grows. Jenkins has written, "Music often calls out an alert response in toddlers—they may even try to dance to a marked rhythm that appeals to them. They often try to turn the radio or television on for themselves" (Jenkins and Shacter 1975, p. 68).

Is there a particular kind of music that commands their attention? Simon's research (1964) with children from nine to thirty-one months of age revealed that strongly rhythmic music evoked the greatest responses, followed by music in which melody predominated. The children he studied responded less frequently to harmonic or dissonant music. Their responses were to the whole, rather than to specific, rhythm or melodies and took the form of body movement, vocal response, or change in facial expression.

In addition to attention to rhythm and melody, very young children also have been found to be attentive to timbre, or tone color. Moorhead and Pond wrote that " . . . the very young child's primary interest is in tone color . . . when he is being a lion he does not sing about a lion, he imitates the lion's voice. . . . It is the *sound* that is important"(1942, pp. 16-17).

A study by Fullard (1967) revealed that three- and four-year-old children, when trained, could identify the violin, clarinet, cello, flute, viola, and French horn when heard in musical contexts. The characteristic sound was the important aspect. This would seem to imply a natural ability and interest among young children to discriminate and conceptualize tone color or timbre.

Allen (reported in Duerkson 1972) similarly studied the attention to instrumental timbre by four- and five-year-olds and found that these children could be trained to discriminate between timbres of varied pairs of instruments, including trombone and French horn, violin and trumpet, flute and violin, cello and bassoon, and oboe and muted trumpet.

Writing of the ability of young children to identify instruments, Moorhead and Pond described this perceptual focus upon timbre:

> As example of the child's perceptions it is interesting to note that we have found the characterizations of the wolf (French horns), the duck (oboe) and the grandfather (bassoon) in Prokofiev's "Peter and the Wolf" to be more easily heard and remembered than the others. That of the cat, which relies for its effect upon melodic sinuosity, seems hardly able to be perceptible to the small child. Here we see that the distinctive timbres of the French horn, oboe and bassoon are what the child perceives and remembers. (1942, p. 17)

Zimmerman has written that the sequence of musical learning for young children should be viewed as " . . . a continuum from assimilation, to accommodation, to discrimination, to categorization, to organization, through improvisation, to the application, and, finally, to the conceptualization—and then the reapplication and the process starts all over again" (1975, p. 20). She writes that two- and three-year-olds need a multiplicity of experiences in assimilating, accommodating, and discriminating, and fewer of the higher order.

With this continuum as a criterion and in light of the studies of children's listening behaviors, the following guidelines are suggested as a basis for planning listening experiences:

♪ Young children are naturally interested in musical sound and tend to respond most markedly to music that is predominantly rhythmic or melodic.

♪ Two- and three-year-old children respond to the whole rather than to specific, isolated aspects of a musical composition.

♪ Movement and vocal imitation are natural outward expressions of attentive listening by young children.

♪ Even very young children have shown a natural ability to perceive and conceptualize tone color, and interest in listening to unfamiliar music may be enhanced by choosing music that is characterized by interesting and/or contrasting instrumental and vocal tone color.

♪ It may be appropriate and rewarding to begin to learn to identify the sound characteristics of standard orchestral, folk, and ethnic instruments with young children.

Young children need to listen to a wide variety of music. Classical and traditional orchestral, vocal, and instrumental music, folk, rock, ethnic, and contemporary popular music—all should be a part of their musical environment. "The child should hear much music, interesting in tone color, short and rhythmically dynamic, played by many different

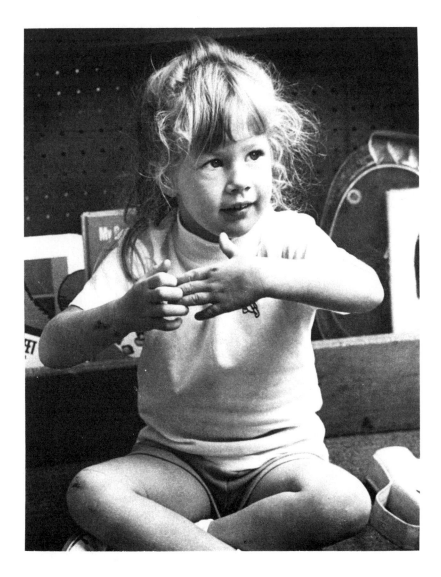

instruments—solo and in small instrumental combinations" (Moorhead and Pond 1942, p. 18).

How can teachers encourage young children to listen to unfamiliar but worthwhile music? McDonald and Schuckert (1968), in attempting to determine whether young children's preferences could be changed by controlled exposure to a less preferred musical selection (classical or jazz), found that nearly fifty percent of the four- to six-year-old children in their study did show a slight change in preference toward the music to which they had been exposed repeatedly. What is best known often is best liked in music.

Teacher approval (Greer, Dorow, and Hanser 1973) also has been cited as an important factor in helping young children recognize, identify, and choose to listen to symphonic music selections in a study concerning young children's preferences before and after discrimination training. Many of you will find that your favorite recorded musical selections, when shared with children, become their favorites also. When you identify for children the musical characteristics of the selection that make it a personal favorite, music teaching is going on.

The many excellent recordings available today that have been planned for children make the task of compiling a library of recordings (children like repetition; a large number of recordings is unnecessary) an easier task than ever before. The RCA series *Adventures in Music* and the *Bowmar Orchestral Library* are two well-known compilations of standard orchestral literature especially chosen for use with children. Bowmar also has *The Small Musician* series for young children. See Appendix B for further information.

Young children need to listen to a wide variety of music. You will find that your favorite recorded musical selections, when shared with children, become their favorites also.

In turn, the contemporary popular sound found in the numerous excellent recordings by Hap Palmer delight young children. Numerous Folkways recordings of folk and ethnic music by artists such as Ella Jenkins are other excellent examples of quality recordings prepared especially for children. Many times, however, children are interested in selections that might seem surprising; one teacher told of a group of four-year-olds' interest in Honegger's "Pacific 231" and of their attempts to illustrate through movement the huge "huffiness" of the locomotive that the music describes.

Because skill in listening is the basis for all musical development, activities that encourage and improve this skill should be planned by teachers. Music in which melody and rhythm are strongly predominant attracts attention and encourages attentive listening. Many interacting factors influence interest in listening to unfamiliar music. Do we, the teachers, enjoy the selection? The children can sense this. Is the selection conducive to some overt response—rhythmic movement, instrumental participation, or children's discussion? Are we eclectic in our choice of records to present to our children? Contemporary pop is fine but should be part of a balanced program. Are we sensitive to which selections children prefer and ask to have repeated; do we keep a record of these choices? What is best known can become best liked. Have we purposefully included selections that will expose children to many types of music?

Four- to six-year-old children

By the time children have reached the age of three and one half or four, they are becoming increasingly social and are ready for more group experiences. They enjoy being with each other, have special friends, and find friends more interesting than adults (Jenkins and Shacter 1975, p. 94). These older children use language well and are fascinated by words. In addition, their sense of humor is tickled by words; they like nonsense rhymes, silly songs, and verses.

> The song, "Don't Throw Your Junk in My Backyard" (see p. 50) was a favorite of one group of four-year-olds. It was a "silly" song to begin with, and the children would end most performances of it with giggles. One day, Lara proposed a new version—"Don't throw your elephant in my backyard; my elephant's there, too!" This version was an immediate hit with the children and many other improvised versions were suggested. Lara's version required fitting in extra syllables in the traditional rhythm of the song. This seemed to add to the popularity of this version!

Seeger, in her song text *American Folk Songs for Children*, has written of such spontaneous improvisations:

> If, when singing a song . . . , you ask children what of their own they would like to sing about you sometimes receive answers which do not fit the rhythm of the song. Traditional singers often insert extra counts to care for such syllables. Children laugh with the pleasure of hearing so many words elbow their way into the middle of a song pattern they know. (1948, p. 28)

Four- and five-year-olds' interest in words offers teachers many opportunities to blend music and language. What can be spoken can be sung, and many times words that are sung are longer remembered than those spoken—how many children have learned letter seriation through the "ABC" song? Older children are ready to learn more about the music itself. Let us consider some of the musical concepts appropriate for these children.

Singing: melodic understandings

With language expanding, singing range is expanding also. To an initial limited singing range used by many young preschoolers, D' to A' (above middle C), notes below middle C are added. Kirkpatrick (1962) reported notes as low as the F below middle C and as high as E (fourth space, treble clef) as within the singing range of four- to six-year-old children.

Some children, however, will still sing songs of wide range with difficulty. Smith (1970) cautioned that by first grade half of the children in a classroom might still be unable to sing accurately in ranges above G' or A'. Accuracy in reproducing melodic intervals increases gradually. Tonal memory is increasing. A feeling for the tonal center of a song is becoming evident; many children who let phrases of a song fall out of key return to the home tone at the conclusion of the song. Not surprisingly, the most tuneful young singers come from home and/or caregiving environments that have provided many experiences and opportunities for singing and listening to music (Kirkpatrick 1962; Young 1971b).

These older children are ready to begin to categorize and organize ideas about the elements of music—melody, rhythm, dynamics, form. Jenkins wrote that five-year-olds " . . . are able to combine ideas and concepts and use them to cope with new situations or to solve simple problems" (Jenkins and Shacter 1975, p. 130). Therefore, the following concepts about **melody** might be introduced.

- Musical sounds may be high or low in pitch.

- Melodies may move up or down or may remain on the same pitch for a number of beats.
- Melodies may move up or down by steps or skips.
- Many melodies move home to a tonal center that may be felt and identified; a satisfactory sense of completion results.
- Certain melodic phrases may be repeated in a song; such repetitions may be recognized and identified.

These concepts are acquired through many experiences in which visual, tactile, and physical movement cues accompany the auditory ones. Even with such training, however, concepts

The most tuneful young singers come from home and/or caregiving environments that have provided many experiences and opportunities for singing and listening to music.

about pitch and melody may remain quite abstract for many children and need frequent reinforcement.

Studies by Williams (1932) and Yendovitskaya (1971) have revealed the importance of visual and/or kinesthetic cueing when introducing concepts about melody. In the Williams study, four- and five-year-old children were trained to associate upward and downward melodic direction in ascending and descending melodies played on the piano with the terms *going upstairs* and *going downstairs*. When asked to demonstrate pitch direction using the piano, all could respond accurately. However, when the visual cueing (keyboard) and kinesthetic (playing) responses were eliminated, the children were less successful. While 90 percent could identify direction when a scale was played, only about half could identify direction of melodic intervals involving steps and smaller skips.

For the four- to six-year-old, we may find it appropriate to introduce songs utilizing a wider pitch range, while still using many spontaneously created songs and limited-range songs. Songs that may be personalized or provide opportunities to change the words to fit the occasion excite interest at this stage of rapid language development.

It is also appropriate to introduce concepts about the various aspects of melody. Children may begin to understand how the terms high-low, steps-skips, up-down, and same-different are used to describe music by associating them with physical movement. Visual and tactile experiences, such as playing phrases or snatches of songs on step bells or song bells, are important to the understanding of these concepts. Teachers may help children stabilize these concepts by habitually tracing the contours of melodies with hand movements (moving their hands up or down in the direction of a melody as the song is sung) and by using the correct terminology when talking with the children about melodies of songs.

Scale songs ("One Potato," for example) may be played on bells to show melodic direction; children can *see* the song move up and down and "come home." Hoops (hula hoops are fine) may be held by three or four children and moved up or down in response to tones or melodies played on a piano or song bells.

Melodic concepts are acquired through many experiences in which visual, tactile, and physical movement cues accompany the auditory ones.

Experimenting with movement and rhythm

Between the ages of four and six, muscular coordination improves, and with it, interest in experimenting with space and movement in rhythmic activities (Christianson 1938, pp. 31-32). These children run, skip, dance, and climb, and are learning to throw and catch a ball. They enjoy rhythm and songs, like to make up dances to music, and enter enthusiastically into singing and rhythmic games (Jenkins and Shacter 1975, p. 126). Christianson (1938) reported the interest of four-year-old children in acting out and dramatizing ideas expressed in music, and stated also that, by the age of five, most children were able to synchronize their movements with rhythmic stimuli. Moog wrote that ". . . if (a child) can keep time by his fourth birthday, he can maintain it for considerably longer periods by age six" (1976, p. 43). He also reported an increased interest in learned movements, like those of singing games and simple dances, at these ages.

The ability to identify and express the beat in music (keeping time) forms the basis for many understandings about the element of rhythm in music, including tempo, durational relationships of notes in rhythmic patterns, accents, and meter groupings. Gell, in a text describing methods of teaching rhythmic movement to young children, stated:

> . . . it is quite certain that we must help cultivate a sense of regular pulsation in the child, if the movement we teach is to be rhythmic, and if the aim is to give musical experience and knowledge. . . .
>
> The automatic action of walking is even, the pulse is even, and the child is surrounded by examples of regular pulsation; therefore it is surely natural that movement should be in time. Teachers must observe with patience that this regularity does not always just "happen," nor does it adjust itself all at once to rhythm outside the child. A very young child cannot immediately respond to a rhythm imposed from an adult. It should never be alarming in the first years that no consistency is shown in regard to this regularity of pulse. It will develop and quite quickly, if care is taken. (1973, p. 45)

Basic rhythmic concepts within the ability of four- to six-year-old children, which grow from their increasing awareness of the beat and ability to express it with music, might include:

- In most music there is an identifiable, underlying steady pulsation—a steady beat.
- Rhythmic beats may be fast or slow, or may get faster or slower.
- Rhythmic patterns may be formed by combining fast and slow beats. Words of songs form rhythmic patterns.
- Certain beats may be accented, and these felt accents help group beats together in twos or threes.
- A song has a rhythmic skeleton. Many songs can be recognized by their rhythm only, without pitch, melody, or words.

The cultivation of the sense of the beat may be through movement, through the use of instruments, or through visual cues such as clocks or metronomes.

Daniel was fascinated with the metronome and liked to move the weight up and down by himself, discussing the resulting differences in speed with the teacher. He was not interested in the teacher's suggestion that he clap "in time" with the beat; he wanted to watch only, and discuss. He was willing, after many such experiences, to adjust the weight in response to the teacher's request, "How can you make the beat go faster—or slower?" Conceptualizing rhythmic beat takes many forms!

Developing rhythmic skills is important to other areas besides music, so there are many sources for helping teachers plan rhythmic activities in an organized way. Cherry's text, *Creative Movement for the Developing Child* (1971), presents a sequential rhythmic program that begins with the most basic of body movements such as wriggling, squirming, crawling, and creeping. Games and activities, accompanied by chants, rhymes, or well-known nursery tunes (with substituted words to fit the activity), are presented to accompany each motor skill. Cherry includes activities for hand and arm movement, finger movement, and leg and foot movement as well as those that require the children to make judgments about the appropriateness of rhythmic responses to certain songs and chants. Directional movement games are also included.

Another excellent text, *Musicbook O* by Bisgaard and Stehouwer (1976), is organized by musical elements; a variety of songs and activities to develop awareness of each element, including rhythm, dynamics, pulse, pitch, and form are included. For teachers with a background in music, Findlay's *Rhythm and Movement: Applications of Dalcroze Eurhythmics* (1971) offers detailed suggestions for teaching young children to express their awareness of the various elements of music through bodily movement. Birkenshaw's *Music for Fun; Music for Learning* (1977) offers many suggestions to teachers for music activities for handicapped as well as very young children. These are examples of but a few of the excellent texts available to teachers.

Four-, five-, and six-year-old children are becoming more skilled at synchronizing movement with the rhythmic beat of music. Action songs, singing games, as well as free, creative movement and simple dances help stabilize this basic rhythmic concept. Tempo still is an important factor in children's ability to synchronize with the beat, and faster tempi for rhythmic experiences may still be easier. Older children can discriminate and verbalize changes of tempi; attention to this element in songs and recorded music can reinforce this understanding. They are also able to understand how combinations of fast and slow sounds make rhythmic patterns, and clapping, drumming the rhythm patterns of their own names, favorite rhymes, chants, poems, and songs help develop awareness of this aspect of rhythm. Basic rhythmic concepts about beat, tempo, and rhythm patterns should be experienced through many activities and a variety of experiences. Research has provided data which suggest that after age nine the most basic rhythmic skill—that of maintaining a steady beat—does not change (or improve) substantially (Zimmerman 1971, p. 25). The development of this skill during the critical stage before age nine would seem to be particularly important.

Instruments: pandemonium or improvisation?

Instruments provide important visual and tactile experiences with all musical elements. Their use in imaginative ways, however, can also help children discover, at their level of understanding, how composers have long used them to create interesting musical compositions.

For example, four- and five-year-old children respond eagerly to stories and poems. They like imaginative stories about animals, about themselves, about experiences familiar to them. They like to make up their own stories. Musical instruments can help illustrate a story and, at the same time, provide opportunities to make judgments that involve knowledge of timbre, dynamics, pitch, rhythm, tempo, and other musical elements. We may start with questions like these: Which instrument could sound like rain on a tin roof? How fast should it be played? How about bears stalking in the woods? How loudly should it be sounded? A child walking through piles of fallen leaves in the autumn? Long or short sounds? A child skipping? Should the sounds be even or uneven? A woodpecker? Fast or slow sounds? One teacher introduced the selection "The Aviary" from the *Carnival of the Animals* by playing for the children a homemade cassette tape recording of sparrows at twilight, twittering as they settled for the night in a bush in the teacher's yard. He then asked the children to choose the instruments that could best be used to imitate these sounds, and then the musical recording was introduced.

So often, simultaneous activity by a large group of children, each with a different instrument, can turn into general pandemonium, and in this kind of atmosphere, children never pay attention to individual sounds or rhythms. With imagination and creative planning, however, instruments may remain the creative outlets for children's imaginative senses that we hope will be their function and, at the same time, further basic musical understandings.

Older children are growing in the ability to understand concepts of pitch, in terms of *high-low, up-down, steps-skips,* and *same.* Opportunities to work with step bells, song bells, and the piano keyboard help them associate pitch with left-to-right direction on these instruments. Often after experimentation, they can play by ear snatches of songs they have learned or, if the song is uncomplicated, the whole melody. "Oh, John the Rabbit," an American folksong found in the Seeger song text, *American Folk Songs for Children,* has a repeated melodic

motif of one tone—on the words "Oh, yes"—which ends each phrase. A single tone bar, removed from the set, makes it easy for a child to answer—"Oh, yes"—in an instrumental rather than singing way.

Similarly, the repeated "ding, ding, dong" motif in the round "Frère Jacques" can be played on two tone bars. These tones, played by the children, can give experience with meanings of higher and lower when describing pitch. "Three Blind Mice" begins with a three-tone motif, which moves downward in steps. "Twinkle, Twinkle, Little Star" allows children to *see* a melodic interval of a "fifth" when they play the beginning phrase. Scalar songs, such as "I Know a Little Pussy," allow opportunity for playing an entire scale. "Rain, Rain, Go Away" can be played on only two or three tone bars.

In addition, playing instruments offers an important medium for creative self-expression. Older children are growing in ability to compose melodies on pitched classroom instruments. Mia's original song notated earlier in this chapter (p. 19) is but one example of interest in this kind of musical activity. Opportunities for such free exploration, improvisation, and invention with instruments should be regarded as prerogatives of all young children. The task of the teacher is to provide an atmosphere where adjustment to the group does not lessen desire to participate, where reasonable authority does not squash creativity, and where the feeling of the group, approval of the teacher, and general atmosphere encourage imagination, alternative ideas, and interest in music-making and music-creating ventures. Andress reminds us that:

> Beautiful equipment may remain
> untouched and unexplored in an overly
> structured atmosphere. . . . The teacher
> must be consistent in allowing all visible
> objects to be touched and played.

Instruments not to be used by the child should be kept out of sight. These instruments should be presented to the child when he is ready to understand and respect their workings. These initial encounters should be planned in order to avoid any unhappy misunderstandings and damage either to the child's feeling toward discovery or to the physical structure of the instrument. It probably would be easier to repair the damage to the instrument than to the child, but it is wise to avoid the need for either. (Andress, Heimann, Rinehart, and Talbert 1973, p. 23-25)

Teachers can provide experiences with timbre by helping children discover, identify, and describe the sounds they hear. The starting point might be the identification of differences between speaking and singing sounds, or the identification of individual children's speaking and singing voices. After these kinds of experiences, differences in percussive sounds of classroom instruments might follow. Then, recordings featuring like groups of instruments, such as string quartets, brass ensembles, piano, organ, harpsichord, or choral music of men's or women's voices could help further understanding of timbre by focusing upon the unique sound produced by such ensembles. At the same time, the manipulative use of instruments in all musical experiences helps stabilize understandings of dynamics, pitch, and rhythm by providing visual and kinesthetic experience with these elements.

With imagination and creative planning, instruments may remain creative outlets for children's imaginative senses and further basic musical understandings.

Concepts concerning timbre, or tone color, that are appropriate for four- to six-year-old children, might include these:

- The unique characteristics of sounds are determined by the type of instrument or voice that produces them.
- Musical instruments may be recognized and identified by their characteristic tone color, or timbre.
- When instruments or voices are used (or played) in different ways, the sound produced by them may be different—e.g., louder, softer, higher, lower, etc.

Appreciating listening

Research in the area of appreciation—which at these ages may be defined as the development of favorable attitudes toward and interest in listening to all kinds of music—has been primarily concerned with older elementary and adolescent children. At the present time, teachers of young children must learn from experience how to plan successfully for listening to unfamiliar music. The guidelines and studies reviewed in "Listening with understanding" (p. 22) should be of interest to those working with four- and five-year-old children as well as younger ones.

Teachers usually find that the longer attention span and ability to listen with more detail, along with a natural interest in stories and dramatic play at these ages, can make music listening time a rewarding experience. For example, four- and five-year-old children enjoy musical stories such as Prokofiev's "Peter and the Wolf." Walt Disney Studios has issued an album that contains a shortened version of this composition and a shortened version of "The Sorcerer's Apprentice," by Dukas, with narration provided.

Most five-year-olds enjoy selections from Saint-Saëns's *Carnival of the Animals;* the titles of the various individual compositions in the suite and the style of the music can inspire them to make up stories about the animals being portrayed musically. One selection—"Cuckoo in the Deep Woods"—became a favorite of one group of children when listening was combined with dramatic play. The teacher preceded the introduction of the music by reading the children a story about a cuckoo clock and cuckoo bird told with some improvisation so that sound effects using rhythm sticks and tone bars could be included. After the children had heard the story, the teacher introduced the recorded selection and suggested that a dramatic interpretation, based on the music, might be created. A most charming interpretation of the music evolved. When the piano theme was heard at the beginning of the selection, the children walked in the woods among the trees (rhythm sticks spaced randomly on the floor). At the end of each piano phrase, when the clarinet played the call of the cuckoo, the children jumped into the nests (hoops lying on the floor among the sticks). When the piano and clarinet themes became intertwined, the children who were baby birds stayed in the nests; the others jumped out. They often asked to enact this musical playlet, they did not seem to tire of repeating it. Each repetition brought forth a suggested refinement based on some hitherto overlooked aspect of the music.

Such detailed listening and interest in the dramatic possibilities of musical compositions is beyond the interest and abilities of most younger children. Four- and five-year-olds, however, found their characteristic interests accommodated and, at the same time, were learning to listen carefully to serious music and to recognize themes, musical motifs, and various instruments.

In an unpublished report of a music listening program using serious music, Turnipseed, Thompson, and Kennedy (1974) reported using similar associative techniques for introducing five-year-old children to classical music.

> Each musical learning experience was initially introduced to the children at the associative level of learning, either by telling a story relating to the work or, later in the year, by relating the new work to prior experiences with familiar works. . . . (p. 2)

These researchers emphasized an active response:

> Each new musical concept was reinforced, usually through some form of overt student involvement. In fact, the programming for attention focus and the overt student involvement in response to the music are two of the most important elements of this structured classical music education program. (p. 2)

As a result of this program, the five-year-old children in this study showed significant gains in auditory skills, including ability to follow directions, and discrimination among word sounds. Of interest was the reported lengthening of the group's attention span for music listening activities. Turnipseed reported that by midyear, the initial 20-minute group activities had been gradually lengthened to 50 minutes (Turnipseed, Thompson, and Kennedy 1974, p. 3). Musical selections used in this study are listed on p. 55.

Care should be taken in a music-movement-story combination so that the music does not get lost in the process. Music for quiet listening is also important—with no interpretive response required. However, the music-movement-dramatic idea combination seems to awaken interest in listening to music throughout the growing-up years. Among the author's memories are a second grade's interpretation of *The Sleeping*

Beauty (Tchaikovsky), the stylized dance created by the male members of a fifth grade class to Saint-Saëns's "Danse Macabre," the story-through-movement interpretation of Strauss's "Til Eulenspiegel" by a sixth grade class (which led to a critical evaluation of the interpretation given this piece by an orchestra at their annual children's concert later in the year), and the interpretation of Bach's "Fugue in G Minor," illustrating fugal form by a group of fifth graders, none of whom had had any dance training. Zimmerman reminds us that " . . . active participation on the part of the children in the musical experience by performing and moving to the music should be sought continually" (1971, p. 20).

Sequence of development

The first half of this chapter focused upon the abilities and responses of very young children. In the latter part of the chapter, the musical behaviors of older children were discussed, along with musical concepts or understandings that would be appropriate for these children.

This is not to suggest that suddenly for four-year-olds music experiences should, or can, become preplanned learning sessions. Quite the contrary. As Andress reminds us: "Because the child is the only one who knows how he perceives things, he must be left in control of his learning. The teacher creates the model; the child determines the aspects to which he will respond" (Andress, Heimann, Rinehart, and Talbert 1973, p. 9). Young children are attracted to learning when the content and method are appropriate, appealing, and attractive. Learning is growing. And, as growing follows more or less sequential stages, so do certain aspects of musical learning. Data from research suggest the following sequence:

- Attention to timbre appears in infancy.
- Perception of loudness (dynamics) appears before the age of four.
- Pitch and rhythmic discriminative abilities appear next, and somewhat concurrently. These abilities are necessarily related to the development of motor coordination, voco-motor control, and tonal memory.
- Perception of harmony develops later, at approximately age eight. Younger children appear to concentrate on melody and/or rhythm and find it difficult to consider the harmonic characteristics of a song or composition. (Zimmerman 1971; Andress, Heimann, Rinehart, and Talbert 1973)

Learning about music, as any kind of learning, depends upon the children's experiences with it, their intellectual capabilities, and their motivation. Parents, teachers, and caregivers play an important role in children's music learning.

> We do not believe that the child can acquire all of his necessary equipment solely by contact with music and musical materials and by free opportunity to create in his own idioms. Certainly in a rich and unregimented environment he habituates himself to the free exercise of creative musicality; he learns many techniques empirically through experimentation and contact with older children who have learned them already, and necessity, for him, is often the mother of invention. But teaching also has its place. (Moorhead and Pond 1942, p. 20)

The music-movement-dramatic idea combination seems to awaken interest in listening to music throughout the growing-up years.

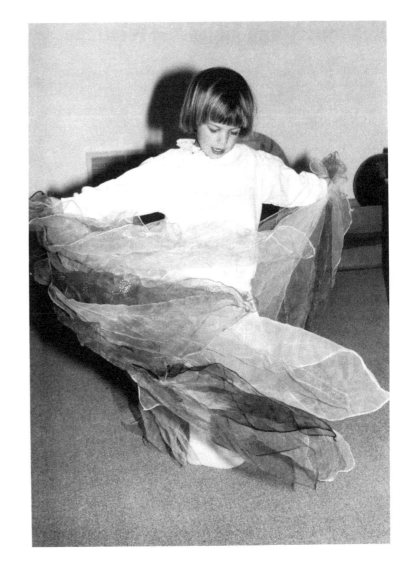

References and suggested readings

Alford, D. L. "Emergence and Development of Music Responses in Preschool Twins and Singletons: A Comparative Study." *Journal of Research in Music Education* 19, no. 2 (Summer 1971): 222-227.

Andress, B. L.; Heimann, H. M.; Rinehart, C. A.; and Talbert, E. G. *Music in Early Childhood*. Reston, Va.: Music Educators National Conference, 1973.

Biasini, A.; Thomas, R.; and Pogonowski, L. *MMCP Interaction: Early Childhood Music Curriculum*. Bardonia, N.Y.: Media Materials, 1970.

Birkenshaw, L. *Music for Fun; Music for Learning*. Toronto: Holt, Rinehart and Winston of Canada, Limited, 1977.

Bisgaard, E., and Stehouwer, G. *Musicbook O*. Edited and adapted by T. Aaron. U.S.A.: Magnamusic/Edition Wilhelm Hansen, 1976.

Cherry, C. *Creative Movement for the Developing Child*. Belmont, Calif.: Lear Siegler/Fearon Publishers, 1971.

Christianson, H. *Bodily Movements of Young Children in Relation to Rhythm in Music*. New York: Columbia University, 1938.

Duerkson, G. L. *Teaching Instrumental Music*. Reston, Va.: Music Educators National Conference, 1972.

Findlay, E. *Rhythm and Movement: Applications of Dalcroze Eurhythmics*. Evanston, Ill.: Summy-Birchard, 1971.

Fullard, W. G., Jr. "Operant Training of Aural Musical Discriminations with Preschool Children." *Journal of Research in Music Education* 15, no. 3 (Fall 1967): 201-209.

Gell, H. *Music, Movement and the Young Child*. Sydney: Australasian Publishing Co., 1973.

Greenberg, M. "Effectiveness of a Music Curriculum with Preschool Head Start Children." *Council for Research in Music Education Bulletin* 29 (Summer 1972): 13-16.

Greer, R. D.; Dorow, L.; and Hanser, S. "Music Discrimination Training and the Music Selection Behavior of Nursery and Primary Level Children." *Council for Research in Music Education Bulletin* 35 (Winter 1973): 30-43.

Ilina, G. A. "On the Formation of Musical Notions in Preschool Age Children." *Child Development Abstracts and Bibliography* 34, no. 3-4 (June-August 1960): 108.

Jenkins, G. G., and Shacter, H. S. *These Are Your Children*. Glenview, Ill.: Scott, Foresman and Co., 1975.

Jersild, A. T., and Bienstock, S. F. *Development of Rhythm in Children*. New York: Columbia University, 1935.

Kirkpatrick, W. C. "Relationships Between the Singing Abilities of Prekindergarten Children and their Home Musical Environment." *Dissertation Abstracts* 23 (1962): 886.

Lind, J., and Hardgrove, C. "Lullabies," *Children Today*, July-August 1978, pp. 7-10, 36.

McDonald, M. "Transitional Tunes and Musical Development." *The Psychoanalytic Study of the Child* 25 (1970): 503-520.

McDonald, R. L., and Schuckert, R. F. "An Attempt to Modify the Musical Preferences of Preschool Children." *Journal of Research in Music Education* 16, no. 1 (Spring 1968): 39-44.

Michel, P. "The Optimum Development of Musical Abilities in the First Years of Life." *Psychology of Music* 1, no. 2 (June 1973): 14-20.

Moog, H. "The Development of Musical Experience in Children of Pre-School Age." *Psychology of Music* 4, no. 2 (1976): 38-45.

Moorhead, G. E., and Pond, D. *Music of Young Children II. General Observations*. Santa Barbara, Calif.: Pillsbury Foundation for Advancement of Music Education, November 1942.

Moorhead, G. E.; Sandvik, F.; and Wight, D. *Music of Young Children IV. Free Use of Instruments for Musical Growth*. Santa Barbara, Calif.: Pillsbury Foundation for Advancement of Music Education, February 1951.

Noy, P. "The Development of Music Ability." *The Psychoanalytic Study of the Child* 23 (1968): 332-347.

Ostwald, P. F. "Musical Behavior in Early Childhood." *Developmental Medicine and Child Neurology* 15, no. 1 (February 1973): 367-375.

Scheihing, G. "A Study of the Spontaneous Rhythmical Abilities of Pre-School Children." *Music Therapy 1950*. Lawrence, Kan.: Allen Press, 1951.

Seeger, R. C. *American Folk Songs for Children*. New York: Doubleday and Co., 1948.

Shelley, S. J. "Music." In *Curriculum for the Preschool-Primary Child—A Review of the Research*, ed. C. Seefeldt. Columbus, Ohio: Charles E. Merrill Publishing Co., 1976.

Shuter, R. *The Psychology of Musical Ability*. London: Methuen and Co., 1968.

Simons, G. M. "Comparisons of Incipient Music Responses Among Very Young Twins and Singletons." *Journal of Research in Music Education* 12, no. 3 (Fall 1964): 212-226.

Smith, R. B. "The Effect of Group Vocal Training on the Singing Ability of Nursery School Children." *Journal of Research in Music Education* 11, no. 2 (Fall 1963): 137-141.

Smith, R. B. *Music in the Child's Education.* New York: Ronald Press Co., 1970.

Turnipseed, J. P.; Thompson, A.; and Kennedy, N. "Utilization of a Structured Classical Music Listening Program in the Development of Auditory Discrimination Skills of Preschool Children." Research Report, 1974.

Voglar, M. "On Musical Creativity." *Predskolsko Dete* 9 (January 1977): 129-143.

Williams, H. M. "Studies in the Rhythmic Performance of Preschool Children." In *The Measurement of Musical Development,* ed. G. D. Stoddard. University of Iowa Studies in Child Welfare, Vol. VII, no. 1 (1932), pp. 32-66.

Yendovitskaya, T. V. "Development of Sensation and Perception." In *The Psychology of Preschool Children,* ed. A. V. Zaporozhets and D. B. Elkonin. Translated by J. Shybut and S. Simon. Cambridge, Mass.: MIT Press, 1971.

Young, W. T. *An Investigation of the Singing Abilities of Kindergarten and First Grade Children in East Texas.* Bethesda, Md.: ERIC Document Reproduction Service, ED 051 252, 1971a.

Young, W. T. *A Study of Remedial Procedures for Improving the Level of Musical Attainment Among Preschool Disadvantaged.* Bethesda, Md.: ERIC Document Reproduction Service ED 051 252, 1971b.

Zimmerman, M. P. *Musical Characteristics of Children.* Reston, Va.: Music Educators National Conference, 1971.

Zimmerman, M. P. "Research in Music Education with Very Young Children." In *Music Education for the Very Young Child. Report of the Fourth International Seminar on Research in Music Education.* Wellington, New Zealand: New Zealand Council for Educational Research, 1975.

3

The Teacher:
Planning Musical Experiences

This book contains information about how young children respond to and use music, in the belief that this kind of information can help us plan appropriate musical experiences for young children. Much of the information derived from studies of the younger children was obtained through careful observation of them in free play or unstructured situations. As children grow and develop skills and understanding through exploration, experimentation, and discovery, they become more interested in group activities, in interpersonal relationships, and in sharing and applying ideas and discoveries in new situations. Throughout these periods, we adults—teachers and parents—play important roles. Our roles change with the needs of the children, the situations that arise spontaneously, and the moods and feelings of the individual children. We need to recognize that planning for music must take into account these human conditions.

Planning for music, however, can be more than a hit and miss procedure. Studies done by psychologists, educators, and music researchers concerning singing songs, spontaneous vocal behavior, rhythmic responses, listening behaviors, and motor abilities offer many guidelines and suggestions to assist us in planning appropriate experiences that will help children enjoyably learn about music.

[Certain musical] facts and techniques must be taught; when and how depends upon the teacher's sensitiveness; the child's need for the knowledge and readiness to learn must decide, for if technical training is in advance of the child's needs it is unassimilable, and produces (as it does in adult musicians)

Guidelines for teaching singing

Singing, movement, and speech are closely related for the very young child, and their combination often results in a chant. We may find opportunities to improvise chants (which match the melodic configurations, repetitive character, and rhythmic movement of those of the children) to musically describe daily occurrences, provide pleasurable ways of moving from one activity to another, and help small children learn what singing is.

When learning songs imitatively, the process of putting together words and pitch often results in restriction of vocal range. We may want to start with songs that utilize children's comfortable range (D to A) and gradually add songs that stretch the ranges to include higher and lower tones.

Since many young children only gradually acquire the ability to match pitches of others, teachers may decide to match the pitches of the children when singing familiar songs.

Growing in ability to categorize and use knowledge from past experiences to understand new experiences, older children can be introduced to concepts about melody in music through singing, by physical motion that correlates with the direction of a song's melody, by visual cues such as dashes or musical notes (not necessarily on a staff) picturing high-low, same, up-down, or by visual/tactile experiences with song bells, piano keyboard, or step bells. Chosen songs should be from a variety of sources, as our children represent many cultures and backgrounds. Therefore, we must not depend upon one song text—there has never been one written to provide adequately for all children. Choose eclectically. Is there "just the song or chant we need" in *Circle Round the Zero: Play Chants and Singing Games of City Children* (Kenney 1975), or *American Folk Songs for Children* (Seeger 1948), or *Step It Down: Games, Plays, Songs, and Stories from the Afro-American Heritage* (Jones and Hawes 1972), or *Musicbook O*—a transplant from Denmark—(Bisgaard and Stehouwer 1976), or *Songs and Stories of the North American Indians* (Glass 1970), or *Children's Songs from Japan* (White and Akiyama 1960), or *Sally Go Round the Sun* (Fowke 1969)? Children know songs, too, that should be shared!

creative sterility. And if the child has technical needs which are not satisfied his creativity is apt to dry up because of his inability to function at his proper level. (Moorhead and Pond 1942, p. 20)

Sometimes we are initiators of musical activities; sometimes participators; sometimes appreciators. Initiating without restricting; participating without unwelcome intervention; appreciating always, with encouragement and caring.

As children grow and develop skills and understanding through exploration, experimentation, and discovery, they become more interested in group activities.

Guidelines for teaching rhythm

For very young children rhythm is an individual experience. Therefore, as teachers, we watch for informal, spontaneous moments when we may imitate rhythms produced by the children and perhaps add a chant, hand clapping, or instrumental accompaniment.

Young children develop the ability to bring their rhythmic responses under control only gradually and through much experience. Therefore we must plan for many opportunities through the day to move spontaneously to music and speech rhythms, without requiring that the movements synchronize with the beat.

Since children learn best using all their senses, instruments, action songs and games, visual devices such as clocks and metronomes, and recordings with predominant rhythmic character are appropriate to develop awareness of the beat and the satisfaction of moving in synch with it.

Older children's greater motor coordination allows them to experiment with rhythmic patterns by clapping and chanting word rhythms of poetry, chant, and song.

Older children are growing in their ability to categorize, organize, and apply previously learned ideas about rhythm. We should encourage improvisation, welcome alternative ideas from the children, and help them verbalize their rhythmic understandings using basic musical terms such as fast-slow, long-short, even-uneven.

Guidelines for using instruments

Young children's natural interest in timbre can be enhanced by allowing much free, exploratory use of instruments to develop awareness of different timbres of pitched and nonpitched sounds.

Instruments are fascinating to young children. We should use them in many ways—to accompany songs, chants, recordings; to help children explore musical concepts such as melodic direction (up, down, same), tempo (fast, slow, getting faster, getting slower), and rhythmic patterns; and to develop imagination in creating original tunes, rhythms, and sounds.

Authentic instruments provide much richer tone quality and are more satisfactory for young children than cheaply made commercial ones. Some percussion instruments, however, can be handmade and still provide acceptable sound and durability.

Guidelines to encourage listening

Adult concepts of what kind of music is appropriate for young children might be restrictive. Therefore we should provide a wide variety of music for listening—classical, jazz, contemporary popular, ethnic music from many cultures, avant-garde, and twentieth century serious music.

We encourage listening to all kinds of music by showing our interest in listening. Selections which are especially enjoyed should be repeated often.

Active listening is more appropriate than passive listening for young children. Children may respond to music with movement, creative dance, or with appropriate instrumental accompaniment. Many times introduction to a musical composition may be through a nonmusical activity, such as a story or free movement without music.

Parents, older children, or other community members provide especially pleasurable listening experiences by bringing not only their music but their personal values of music making to the children. They should be invited often.

We watch for informal, spontaneous moments when we may imitate rhythms produced by the children and perhaps add a chant, hand clapping, or instrumental accompaniment.

Methods for teaching music

Alford has stated that during the early years patterns of response are formulated that will influence all future growth and development in music.

> It is evident . . . that (a) children do respond to music and are capable at a very early age of doing more musically than educators have previously admitted; (b) growth, experience, and training do affect young children's response to music; and (c) some experiences, as seen in current teaching, can be presented profitably much earlier than was previously thought. It is therefore also evident that music educators should seriously consider formulating a program to initiate significant music education experiences and training as early as possible with every child. This probably will necessitate the development of more effective kindergarten and nursery school programs. . . . (1971, p. 227)

There has been much recent interest in a number of methodologies whose originators have considered the early years as the logical starting time for music education. Perhaps the best known of the methods are those of Dalcroze, Kodàly, Orff, Suzuki, and the program known as the MMCP. Many of the basic doctrines of these methods are not new, but it is important to be acquainted with the methods and techniques used to teach music to young children.

The Dalcroze Method, originated by Emile Jaques-Dalcroze, a Swiss composer and music educator, emphasizes body movement, ear training, and improvisation by the teacher at the piano to awaken children's awareness of musical elements. Rhythmic movement to music, eurhythmics, is the basic approach of this method. Many of Jaques-Dalcroze's procedures have been adopted by music educators throughout the world. A comprehensive bibliography of books, articles, and studies of this method, as well as a general description of the method can be found in *The Eclectic Curriculum in American Music Education: Contributions of Dalcroze, Kodàly and Orff* by Landis and Carder (1972).

The Kodàly Method, also described in the Landis-Carder book, was originated by Zoltán Kodàly, a Hungarian composer

Parents, older children, or other community members provide especially pleasurable listening experiences by bringing not only their music but their personal value of music making to the children.

and music educator. This method is essentially a vocal approach to music education. "Reading and writing musical notation are primary goals in the Kodàly system" (Landis and Carder 1972, p. 44), and such training begins in the early childhood years. Kodàly approaches vocal sight singing through the "Movable 'do'" system in which individual pitches with their syllable names are introduced in a definite sequential order. Beginning with the "teasing chant" of childhood, first songs employ only these two syllables, sol and mi; their relative relationship (and all other pitches as well) is reinforced by body movement describing the melodic direction and later transcribed to hand signals—each pitch represented by a specific hand position. Rhythm patterns are also introduced in an ordered sequence of difficulty, and a simplified stick notation is used for first reading and writing of rhythm patterns. Many of the songs used by Kodàly are found in Hungarian folk literature; in addition, he composed a song text for very young children entitled *Fifty Nursery Songs*. Choksy has adapted the system using American folksongs in *The Kodàly Method*. Richards has also published a series of songbooks and charts based on this method, entitled *Threshold to Music*.

The approach used by Carl Orff, a German composer and music educator, is based on the idea that music, speech, and movement should be combined when teaching music to young children. Creative improvisation by the children is emphasized. All activities in this approach call for improvisation—through movement, speech, and on specially designed instruments. Xylophones, metallaphones, and glockenspiels with removable tone bars enable children to improvise accompaniments, introductions, and codas to songs by using only a limited number of tones.

Both Orff and Kodàly use pentatonic song literature in beginning instruction. Pentatonic songs use only five tones of a diatonic scale, eliminating the fa (fourth step of the scale) and the ti (seventh step). (The sound of this scale can be realized by playing only the black keys of a piano.) Accompaniments employing motifs from pentatonic melodies are created by the children in these methods. Landis and Carder provide a bibliography and comprehensive discussion of this method in *The Ecclectic Curriculum in American Music Education*.

The MMCP program, entitled *MMCP Interaction: Early Childhood Music Curriculum*, is an early childhood learning plan produced by the Manhattanville Music Curriculum Program (USOE 6 - 1999) and developed in 1965-1970. *Interaction* is described as a process-oriented curriculum based on the belief that personal involvement in the process of making music is the way young children learn about music. Through a series of phases—Free Exploration; Guided Exploration; Exploratory Improvisation; Planned Improvisation; Reapplication—young children learn to manipulate sounds, both musical and nonmusical, organize and classify them, use them in expressive and aesthetically satisfying ways, and reapply them in ways to express many different moods and feelings.

> In this creative program extensive use is made of a wide variety of recordings. These are used to provide musical clues for the child, to assist him to find answers to his own creative problems. Such questions as "How can I add more variety to my piece?" "How do pieces end?" are often answered far better with examples from the literature than by verbal explanations by the teacher. (Biasini, Thomas, and Pogonowski 1970, p. 35)

A special approach to teaching the violin has been developed by **Shinichi Suzuki** in Japan (Kendall 1973). In the original form of the method, it is a special style of individual instruction, with parents of the young students involved in the instruction. In Japan, for example, all mothers receive about three months of violin instruction before the child begins on the instrument. Young pupils begin instruction on miniature instruments. Each lesson is audited by a parent, who then is able to supervise the following week's practice. All music is taught by rote in the beginning stages, with much listening and direct imitation of the teacher. Pupils are brought together for festivals where they play in unison the various compositions they have learned and memorized.

Only brief, and admittedly incomplete, descriptions of these methods have been presented; complete descriptions and discussions of them may be found in the sources cited at the end of the chapter. Each method offers its own unique philosophy and approach. They have in common, however, the goal of all methods for teaching music to young children—making music a meaningful and vital dimension in the life of every young child.

References and suggested readings

Alford, D. L. "Emergence and Development of Music Responses in Preschool Twins and Singletons: A Comparative Study." *Journal of Research in Music Education* 19, no. 2 (Summer 1971): 222-227.

Biasini, A.; Thomas, R.; and Pogonowski, L. *MMCP Interaction: Early Childhood Music Curriculum.* Bardonia, N.Y.: Media Materials, 1970.

Bisgaard, E., and Stehouwer, G. *Musicbook O.* Edited and adapted by T. Aaron. U.S.A.: Magnamusic/Edition Wilhelm Hansen, 1976.

Choksy, L. *The Kodály Method.* Englewood Cliffs, N.J.: Prentice-Hall, 1974.

Fowke, E. *Sally Go Round the Sun.* New York: Doubleday and Co., 1969.

Glass, P. *Songs and Stories of the North American Indians.* New York: Grosset and Dunlap, 1970.

Jones, B., and Hawes, B. L. *Step It Down: Games, Plays, Songs, and Stories from the Afro-American Heritage.* New York: Harper and Row, 1972.

Kendall, J. D. *What the American Music Educator Should Know about Shinichi Suzuki.* Reston, Va.: Music Educators National Conference, 1973.

Kenney, M. *Circle Round the Zero: Play Chants and Singing Games of City Children.* St. Louis, Mo.: Magnamusic-Baton, 1975.

Kodály, Z. *Fifty Nursery Songs.* U.S.A.: Boosey and Hawkes, 1964.

Landis, B., and Carder, P. *The Eclectic Curriculum in American Music Education: Contributions of Dalcroze, Kodály and Orff.* Reston, Va.: Music Educators National Conference, 1972.

Moorhead, G. E., and Pond, D. *Music of Young Children. I: General Observations.* Santa Barbara, Calif.: Pillsbury Foundation for Advancement of Music Education, November 1942.

Richards, M. H. *Threshold to Music.* Belmont, Calif.: Fearon Publishers, 1964.

Seeger, R. C. *American Folk Songs for Children.* New York: Doubleday and Co., 1948.

White, F., and Akiyama, K. *Children's Songs from Japan.* New York: Edward B. Marks Music Corp., 1960.

4

Children's Music

Included in this last chapter are some of the songs created by children with whom I have worked, as well as some songs that were most popular with these children. The spontaneous or original songs presented first are representative of many that were tape recorded. They are notated at the exact pitch levels the children used. The children were engaged in play activities and were completely unaware that their tunes were being recorded. The additional songs in this chapter, those most popular among the groups of children I have known, are preceded or followed by observations of some of the musical characteristics of the songs and by anecdotal comments about the children's use of, or reactions to, the songs. All songs are pitched in the tonalities the children found easiest for singing.

Spontaneous songs

Whether or not teachers of young children include music in their daily curriculum, it nonetheless is there. It is there because children are there, and they bring with them their interest in making music.

Five-year-old Amy sang this tune one day on two separate occasions. Teachers might use it to effect smooth transition between activities, as suggested by the substituted words in parentheses.

One, two, three, and a-way we go;

Ho, ho, ho, ho, ho!

(or) Time for snacks ho, ho!

(or) Now it's time to go!

Jimmy (age three years, four months) sang this little tune over a number of days as he scaled a set of climbing bars in a corner of the room. This one, also, could be used for a transition between activities or to accompany children's movement in groups from one place to another (with substituted words).

Walk-ing up the stairs; walk-ing up the stairs!

The following song was repeated over and over again by its composer, Carl (age two years, six months) as he played with a group of children who were busy with clay.

Roll, roll, roll, roll, roll, roll, roll, roll,

roll, roll, roll, roll, roll, roll, roll, roll, roll, roll, roll, roll.

The only pentatonic tune recorded was the familiar "teasing chant" presented on the next page. It, however, was the most frequently heard spontaneous song. It was sung in almost every tonality, beginning on such widely contrasting pitch levels as the A below middle C to the E, fourth space, treble clef. All performances were intervallically accurate and sung with energy. This was not a song for quiet, introspective, individual play, as the various words used by different children indicate.

No   one can find   me!   Boing, boing, bong-bong, boing!
Dum   did - dy dum   dum!   (pounding blocks)
Andy took a - nother one!
We   do - n't care   – !
I   found a lady   bug!

Limited-range songs: action songs for very young children

Younger children sing most comfortably in a range from approximately D to A above middle C. Action songs that encourage young children to explore and enjoy ways of moving rhythmically in their own ways are more appropriate than those requiring synchronization with the beat.

Younger children sing most comfortably in a range from D to A above middle C. Action songs are more appropriate than those requiring synchronization with the beat.

"Teddy Bear," a traditional rope-jumping chant from childhood, is built upon the teasing chant melodic configuration. It also provided large-muscle actions that were fun for the younger children. We used this version:

Teddy Bear

(Traditional)

Ted - dy bear, ted-dy bear, turn a - round; ted - dy bear, ted - dy bear, touch the ground. Ted - dy bear, ted-dy bear, show your shoe;

ted - dy bear, ted - dy bear, be ex - cused. Ted - dy bear, ted-dy bear, turn out the light; ted - dy bear, ted - dy bear, say good - night!

After the song was well learned, two tone bars, G and E, were removed from the full set, and a child played "Teddy Bear" whenever it occurred. This was no simple task, but it was fun, and if we goofed, no one cared!

This untitled song sort of grew with the group. Its tune resembles the "Hokey Pokey," but is its own invention. In it, the actions suggested by the words give physical demonstration of the melodic direction of the tune. The range stretched that of many of our youngest children.

I put my arms up high; I put my arms down low; I

shake my arms when they're up high and then I let them go!

We then tried *feet, shoulders,* and *heads* for alternate versions.

"Twinkle, Twinkle, Little Star" seems to be known by almost every young child! We played it on song bells, traced the melodic contour with whole-body movement, hand movement, and sang all the other versions we had learned from parents, big brothers, and sisters! We usually let individual children pitch it for the rest of us, and they usually started it on middle C, D, or E.

Twin - kle, twin - kle, lit - tle star, how I won - der

what you are. Up a - bove the world so high,

like a dia - mond in the sky. Twin - kle, twin - kle,

lit - tle star, how I won - der what you are!

Many of the younger children, who all seemed to have learned the alphabet with this song, compressed the beginning interval to a third (starting on F instead of D). The words for the alphabet were sung like this:

A, B, C, D,——E, F, G.——H, I, J, K,——L, M, N, O, P.
Q, R, S———T, U, V—W, X,———Y, Z,
Tell me what you think of me;
I can say my A B C's.

One of the children, a four-year-old, had learned another version from her sister and she introduced it to the group. It was an instant hit!

> Twinkle, Twinkle, little bat,
> How I wonder where you're at!
> Up above the world so high,
> Like a platter in the sky,
> Twinkle, Twinkle, little bat,
> How I wonder where you're at!

Silly songs

Older children use language well and are fascinated by words. Many times their sense of humor is infectious; they like nonsense rhymes, silly songs, and verses.

Improvising on the words in songs often makes older children laugh. "Don't Throw Your Junk" was one such song. The children delighted in fitting substitute words where the word *junk* occurred; we found that everything from *elephants* to *kangaroos* fitted into this slot!

Don't Throw Your Junk

(Source Unknown)

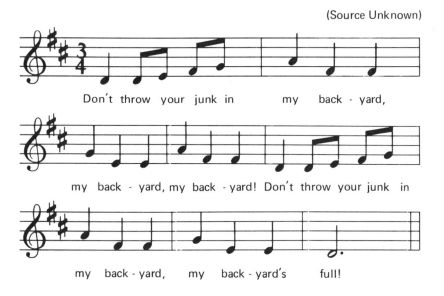

Don't throw your junk in my back - yard, my back - yard, my back - yard! Don't throw your junk in my back - yard, my back - yard's full!

"Miss Merry Mack" has an easily-sung melody and limited range; its silly words made this one a favorite of older children. The version we liked was in *Circle Round the Zero,* a collection of songs by Maureen Kenney. We clapped our hands with the beat as we sang it.

Miss Merry Mack*

(Traditional Children's Game)

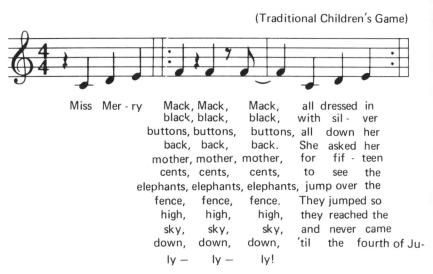

Miss Mer - ry Mack, Mack, Mack, all dressed in
black, black, black, with sil - ver
buttons, buttons, buttons, all down her
back, back, back. She asked her
mother, mother, mother, for fif - teen
cents, cents, cents, to see the
elephants, elephants, elephants, jump over the
fence, fence, fence. They jumped so
high, high, high, they reached the
sky, sky, sky, and never came
down, down, down, 'til the fourth of Ju-
ly — ly — ly!

*From *Circle Round the Zero: Play Chants and Singing Games of City Children,* by Maureen Kenney. © Maureen Kenney, Magnamusic-Baton, 1975, St. Louis. Used by permission.

Laura, age four, provided an improvised ending or coda that the children thought was fine!

Ne - ver a - gain, ne - ver a - gain, ne - ver a - gain!

Singing games and action songs for older children

> If a child can keep time by his fourth birthday, he can maintain it for considerably longer periods of time. . . . [Children over four] show an increased interest in learned movements, like those of singing games and dances, at these ages. (Moog 1976, p. 43)

Introduced for Valentine's Day, "Big Bunch of Roses" became a favorite of four- and five-year-olds. They liked the funny words and the dancelike actions. Finding the original key too high, we transposed the melody.

Big Bunch of Roses*

Folk Game Song
Collected by John W. Work

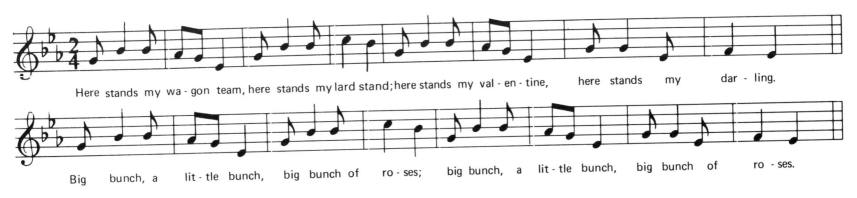

Here stands my wa-gon team, here stands my lard stand; here stands my val-en-tine, here stands my dar-ling.

Big bunch, a lit-tle bunch, big bunch of ro-ses; big bunch, a lit-tle bunch, big bunch of ro-ses.

---

*Melody and words from *Music in Our Town,* by Mursell, Tipton, Landeck, Nordholm, Freeburg, and Watson. © 1962 by Silver Burdett Co. Reprinted by permission of Mrs. John W. Work III.

One child, holding a chiffon scarf, skipped around the other children who were spaced randomly. On the word *darling*, the child floated the scarf over the head of the nearest child. They held hands, and the two of them skipped around while the children sang and clapped the last eight measures beginning with the words *Big bunch*. Then the newly-chosen child took the scarf and started the game once again.

After Valentine's Day had long passed, we were still singing and playing this game-song with gusto!

Many times, music can help young children acquire, or reinforce, nonmusical concepts such as directionality, body parts identification, color recognition, or number and letter seriation. A song makes fun the necessary repetition for learning these. The song, "Head and Shoulders, Baby," was one of the all-time favorites of both younger and older children. We added verses that named other parts of our bodies that were next to each other. Our version was found in *Step It Down: Games, Plays, Songs, and Stories from the Afro-American Heritage*, by Jones and Hawes. We used the first and last sections of the song to avoid too much wordiness. It seemed to go better in this key than the one given in the song text, so we sang it in this higher key.

Head and Shoulders, Baby*

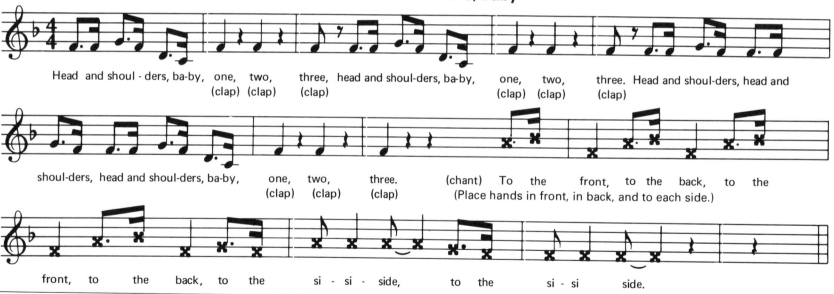

*Words and music by Bessie Jones. Collected and edited with additional new material by Alan Lomax TRO—© 1972 Ludlow Music, Inc., New York. Used by permission.

Using instruments with songs

The use of instruments can provide important visual and tactile experiences with auditory phenomena that otherwise can remain quite abstract.

Softly, Softly*

German Folk Tune

Soft - ly,   soft - ly,   make no   noise at   all.

Soft - ly,   soft - ly,   make no   noise at   all.

Qui - et,   now we   want to sleep.   Qui - et,   now we   want to sleep.

Soft - ly,   soft - ly,   make no   noise at   all.

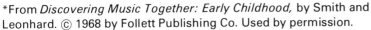

*From *Discovering Music Together: Early Childhood,* by Smith and Leonhard. © 1968 by Follett Publishing Co. Used by permission.

After the song had been learned, a chart was prepared that looked like this:

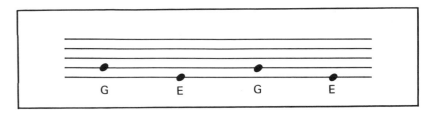

G   E   G   E

Two tone bells, G and E, were removed from the full set. The children took turns playing the melody pattern for the words *Softly, Softly.* Another child pointed to the notes when they were played. No attempt was made to read lines and spaces or to teach music reading. However, older children are becoming increasingly interested in symbols—letters, numbers, words. Their interest extends to the symbols that represent musical sounds. We prepared charts for various other songs featuring prominent melodic motifs—songs we knew were favorites of the children.

The children also changed the words of the second phrase of the song to *Quiet while the baby sleeps*—perhaps describing a situation closer to their experience!

One of the "instruments" our older children used to develop feeling for a steady beat was a large red ball, good for bouncing. We made up a chant/game that was enjoyed by all the children.

Ball-Bouncing Rhyme

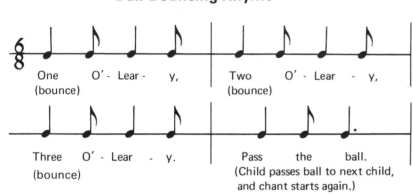

One O'-Lear - y,
(bounce)

Two O'-Lear - y,
(bounce)

Three O'-Lear - y.
(bounce)

Pass the ball.
(Child passes ball to next child, and chant starts again.)

Eventually we added a song:

(Source Unknown)

Boun - cy, boun - cy bal - ly, drib - ble - y, drob - ble - y, whoop - si - dai - sy! Boun - cy, boun - cy, bal - ly, drib - ble - y, drob - ble - y dray. I'm smart, doo-dle-y do, so smart, doo-dle-y do, I knew how to bounce it from the start, doo-dle-y do —,

Fine

D.S. al Fine

54

"Let's sing." Let us hope that these words are heard often, and received with enthusiasm by young children. To sing is to use one's most intimate musical instrument—one's voice. How can a child grow without learning to use this instrument?

Classical music: a starting point

Children respond to the music they hear in their own way and at their own level. In later years they will respond to this same music in different ways. Of course, the music remains the same, but they are different; and since they are in a gradual process of maturing, their later responses will be correspondingly more mature. . . . There is much music which is too difficult for (children) to perform, but there is none too good for them to hear. (Gary 1967, p. 157)

Many suggestions for recordings, appropriate for use with children, have been given throughout this book. Listed below, however, are the selected musical compositions identified by Turnipseed (Turnipseed, Thompson, and Kennedy 1974) in the study of the effect of a structured classical music listening program on the development of auditory discrimination skills in young children. Some of these compositions are included in either the *Adventures in Music* or *Bowmar Orchestral Library* series. This list is not meant to be restrictive; rather, it may serve as a starting point for choosing classical music for a record collection. To it should be added music of very early and contemporary periods and music of other cultures.

Debussy, C.: "Golliwog's Cakewalk" from the *Children's Corner Suite*.
Coates, E.: *Cinderella*.
Donaldson, H.: "The Three Billy Goats Gruff" and "The Little Train" from the *Once Upon a Time Suite*.
Tchaikovsky, P.: *The Nutcracker Suite*.
Dukas, P.: *The Sorcerer's Apprentice*.
Jurey, E. B.: *Brother John and the Village Orchestra*.
Saint-Saëns, C.: *Carnival of the Animals*.
Grofé, F.: *The Grand Canyon Suite*.
Saint-Saëns, C.: *Danse Macabre*.
Mussorgsky, M., and Ravel, M.: *Pictures at an Exhibition*.

The treasures of the art of music are found in its literature. This literature—both of the past and of the present—is so pervasive a part of the total cultural heritage that it is a basic obligation of education to pass this heritage on to succeeding generations. (Gary 1967, p. 157)

References and suggested readings

Gary, C. L., ed. *The Study of Music in the Elementary School—A Conceptual Approach*. Reston, Va.: Music Educators National Conference, 1967.
Jones, B., and Hawes, B. L. *Step It Down: Games, Plays, Songs, and Stories from the Afro-American Heritage*. New York: Harper and Row, 1972.
Kenney, M. *Circle Round the Zero: Play Chants and Singing Games of City Children*. St. Louis, Mo.: Magnamusic-Baton, 1975.
Moog, H. "The Development of Musical Experience in Children of Pre-School Age." *Psychology of Music* 4, no. 2 (1976): 38-45.
Mursell, J. L.; Tipton, G.; Landdeck, B.; Nordholm, H.; Freeburg, R. E.; and Watson, J. M. *Music in Our Town*. Morristown, N.J.: Silver Burdett Co., 1962.
Turnipseed, J. P.; Thompson, A.; and Kennedy, N. "Utilization of a Structured Classical Music Listening Program in the Development of Auditory Discrimination Skills of Pre-School Children." Research Report, 1975.
Weske, E. B. *Exploring Music: Kindergarten*. New York: Holt, Rinehart and Winston, 1969.

A

Glossary of Musical Terms

Beat. Recurrent throb or pulse in music.

Cadence. The beat of rhythmic motion.

Coda. An ending to a musical composition that is added as a conclusion.

Dynamics. Degrees of sound-volume—e.g., loud, soft, getting louder, etc.

Form. Overall design or structure on which a musical work is constructed.

Harmony. The vertical aspect of music; e.g., the effect created when two or more tones are sounded simultaneously.

Improvisation. Process of making up music at the moment, without previous planning.

Interval. Distance from one pitch to another. For example, the distance from middle C to the F above could be described as a *fourth.*

Melodic rhythm. Rhythmic patterns formed by the words and/or melody of a song or composition.

Melody. A succession of musical tones; the horizontal aspect of music contrasted with *harmony,* the vertical aspect.

Meter. Grouping of rhythmic beats into regular patterns of accented and unaccented beats. The two most common groupings (meters) are in two's (duple) and three's (triple).

Pitch. Highness or lowness of a sound.

Rhythm. Aspects of music having to do with time; for example, meter, tempo, and patterns of long and short durational values found in a musical passage.

Scale. A series of pitches ascending and descending according to a prescribed pattern of intervals.

Skip. A melodic interval wider than one whole step.

Step. A melodic interval of one whole tone—e.g., from C to D is a step.

Tempo. The speed of music.

Timbre. Characteristic tone quality of a voice or instrument, also termed *tone color.*

Tonal center. The note that conveys the feeling of a home tone or key center; also, the beginning and ending tone of a scale.

Transposition. Writing or performing a melody in a key or tonality other than the one in which it was written.

B

Resource Materials

Songbooks and musical guides

There are a number of useful songbooks and teachers' guides for musical activities for young children. The following list is a selective one, representative of the materials currently available.

Aaron, Tossi, ed. **Music for Children Volume 1: Preschool.** Orff-Schulwerk American Edition. Corey Field Publishers, P.O. Box 850, Valley Forge, PA 19482. 1982.

A teacher's guide to the Orff-Schulwerk approach to musical learning. Contains chants, games, pieces for dramatic play, songs, and articles about the method. Ideas for body percussion and/or simple percussion and Orff instrumental accompaniments are given.

Beall, Pamela, and Nipp, Susan. **Wee Sing** (series). Price/Stern/Sloan Publishers, Inc., 11150 Olympic Blvd., 6th Floor, Los Angeles, CA 90064.

The **Wee Sing** series songbooks contain traditional children's songs, rhymes, chants, and fingerplays. Each book is accompanied by a cassette tape of its contents. Included in the series are

"Wee Sing"
"Wee Sing and Play"
"Wee Sing Silly Songs"
"Wee Sing for Christmas"
"Wee Sing Nursery Rhymes and Lullabies"

Birkenshaw, Lois. **Music for Fun: Music for Learning.** Holt, Rinehart and Winston of Canada, Toronto, Canada. 1977.

Songs, rhymes, games, and rhythmic activities for children in regular primary and early childhood classrooms and children in special education classes. The activities are fun to do and are designed to help develop motor and auditory skills and musical concepts through songs, dances, rhythms, and speech games. Activities and songs are categorized by topics such as spatial relationships, speech skills, body awareness, and shape perception. A very useful text, well organized and full of good ideas.

Bisgaard, Erling, and Stehouwer, Gulle. **Musicbook O.** Magnamusic/Edition Wilhelm Hansen, 10370 Page Industrial Blvd., St. Louis, MO 63132. 1976.

A songbook and teacher's guide that offers a variety of musical activities and experiences for young children. The book is organized around basic musical concepts such as pulse, sound/silence, dynamics, pitch, rhythm, and form. These are delightful songs and games with piano accompaniments and chord symbols for auto-harp or guitar. Visual aids for the games and activities are included.

Bley, Edgar S. **Best Singing Games for Children of All Ages.** Sterling Publishing Co., Inc., 2 Park Ave., New York, NY 10016. 1976.

A collection of singing games classified for three age groups—preschool and kindergarten, primary grades, and elementary school grades. Included are folksongs and games from all over the world, with teaching suggestions for each. Good fun.

Bradford, Louise Larkins. **Sing It Yourself: 220 Pentatonic Folk Songs.** Alfred Publishing Co., Inc., Box 5964, 15335 Morrison St., Sherman Oaks, CA 91413. 1978.

A collection of American folk melodies using a limited range of tones. Only melodies for the songs are given; accompaniments are not included. The book contains folksongs from many different states in the United States as well as several foreign-text songs that are well known in America. Suggestions for hand-clapping accompaniments for many individual songs are provided. The songs are classified according to their melodic range—for example, from "Songs Within the Compass of a Third and Fourth," "Songs Within the Compass of a Fifth," to "Songs Within the Compass of a Tenth and Eleventh." Collections such as this may be used with the Kodàly and Orff methods; however, these attractive songs (particularly those within the smaller range compasses) are fine to use with very young children whether or not such methods are used.

Commins, Dorothy Berliner. **The Big Book of Favorite Songs for Children.** Grosset & Dunlap, Inc., 200 Madison Ave., New York, NY 10016. 1951.

This collection contains 29 favorite songs of early childhood.

Edmund, Doris. **Let's Begin with a Song.** Creative Teaching Press, Inc., Monterey Park, CA. 1975.

The purpose of this book is to provide suggestions and ideas for exploring many topics of interest to young children, such as animals, the seasons and weather, our bodies, and special days and holidays. Short songs about each topic (with melodies composed by the author or with texts that may be sung to familiar nursery tunes) are included to generate enthusiasm, participation, and personal involvement in each topic. Many suggested activities for each topic are provided. This book provides ideas for ways to include music in traditional curriculum areas and is particularly useful for teachers having a limited musical background. Piano accompaniments are provided.

Feierabend, John. **Music for Little People** and **Music for Very Little People.** Boosey and Hawkes, 52 Cooper Square, New York, NY 10003.

Each book contains authentic folk songs and rhythmic activities of young children. For preschoolers is **Music for Little People; Music for Very Little People** is for teachers and caregivers of infants and toddlers. A cassette tape accompanies each book.

Fowke, Edith. **Sally Go Round the Sun.** Doubleday and Co., Inc., 501 Franklin Ave., Garden City, NY 11530. 1969.

A collection of songs, rhymes, rope-skipping chants, and children's street games from Canada and the United States. Many can be used successfully with young children. Teachers will find here many of the playground rhymes, songs, and games remembered from their own childhood, but seldom found in print.

Gelineau, R. Phyllis. **Songs in Action.** McGraw-Hill Book Co., 1221 Avenue of the Americas, New York, NY 10020. 1974.

An extensive collection of traditional, folk, and composed songs and accompanying activities classified by age/grade levels. Piano accompaniments and chord symbols for autoharp or guitar are provided. Many of the songs and suggested activities are appropriate for young children.

Glazer, Tom. **Eye Winker, Tom Tinker, Chin Chopper: Fifty Musical Fingerplays.** Doubleday and Co., Inc., 501 Franklin Ave., Garden City, NY 11530. 1973.

A delightful collection of songs and fingerplay activities, many of which are appropriate for young children. Piano accompaniments and chord symbols for guitars or autoharps are provided. There are many familiar fingerplay songs as well as some new ones composed for the text, along with well-known folksongs with new fingerplay accompaniments.

Jones, Bessie, and Hawes, Bess Lomax. **Step It Down: Games, Plays, Songs, and Stories from the Afro-American Heritage.** Harper & Row, 10 East 53rd St., New York, NY 10022. 1972.

The songs, games, and plays in this text are the recollections of Bessie Jones, born and raised in Georgia some seventy years ago. The book is divided into sections: baby games and plays, clapping plays, jumps and skips, singing plays, ring plays, dances, house plays and amusements, outdoor games, and songs and stories. Mrs. Jones's introductions to the songs and stories give a vital perspective to this important folk material. Many of the songs and activities are appealing to young children.

McLaughlin, Roberta, and Wood, Lucille. **Sing a Song of People.** Bowmar Publishing Co., Los Angeles, CA. 1973.

A collection of 75 songs classified in units about holidays and seasons, home and community, and neighbors. The songs were chosen to promote language expression and develop motivation for musical expression through movement. Autoharp accompaniments and teaching suggestions for many of the traditional, composed, and folksongs are included.

McLaughlin, Roberta, and Wood, Lucille. **The Small Singer Songbook.** Bowmar Publishing Co., Los Angeles, CA. 1969.

This book contains 125 familiar and composed songs for young children to sing. Piano accompaniments and chord symbols for autoharp are included. Teachers will find songs for special days and seasons, songs for practicing cognitive skills such as counting and color identification, songs which lend themselves to dramatization, action games, and songs which are for fun and relaxation. This book is part of *The Small Musician* series, which includes five recordings in addition to this song text.

Music Resource Book. Augsberg Fortress, 2900 Queen Ln., Philadelphia, PA 19129. 1967.

A collection of traditional songs with suggested activities for informal and creative experiences with rhythmic movement, improvised singing and singing games, and simple fun and folksongs. Although prepared for teachers involved in religious education, this book contains resources and teaching suggestions useful to all early childhood teachers. Piano accompaniments and chord symbols for autoharp or guitar are provided for each song.

Palmer, Hap. **The Hap Palmer Songbook: Learning Basic Skills Through Music, Vol. 1.** Educational Activities, Inc., 1937 Grand Ave., Baldwin, NY 11510. 1971.

This songbook contains many of the songs, so popular with children and teachers, found in the Hap Palmer recordings for children with a contemporary "pop" sound. Chord symbols for guitar accompaniment are provided.

Seeger, Ruth Crawford. **American Folk Songs for Children.** Doubleday and Co., Inc., 501 Franklin Ave., Garden City, NY 11530. 1948.

A collection of 90 American folksongs with piano accompaniments and chord symbols for autoharp. Introductory chapters of this text provide information, suggestions, and tips about how to sing the songs, how to improvise the words, and how to introduce the songs to children. In addition, the reader is given a "feel" for the humor and play of these folksongs and an understanding of their importance as part of our cultural heritage.

Wirth, Marian; Stassevitch, Verna; Shotwell, Rita; and Stemmler, Patricia. **Musical Games, Fingerplay and Rhythmic Activities for Early Childhood.** Parker Publishing Co., West Nyack, NY.

Written for classroom teachers, this book is a collection of time-tested songs, chants, fingergames, circle games, and follow-the-leader games. For each song activity, a suggested age-level is given. Because all the games and activities are meant to be performed in a group, social skills are developed.

Music book series

Each of the major publishers of music series textbooks publishes a text for kindergarten music; some have one for early childhood music. Each is a resource collection of songs, rhythmic activities, listening activities, instrumental activities, and songs for special times. The following series texts are representative of these comprehensive early childhood music guides. Recordings of the songs and compositions included in these texts are available for most of the books.

GIA Publications, Inc.
7404 So. Mason Ave.
Chicago, IL 60638

Jump Right In by David G. Woods and Edwin E. Gordon. Based on Gordon's Learning Theory.

Holt, Rinehart & Winston
383 Madison Ave.
New York, NY 10017

Holt Music by Eunice Boardman and Barbara Andress. A comprehensive music curriculum.

Macmillan/McGraw Hill Publishers
Front and Brown Streets
Riverside, NJ 08075

Music and You by Barbara Staton and Merrill Staton, eds. A comprehensive music curriculum.

Silver Burdett and Ginn
Customer Service Center
4343 Equity Drive
P.O. Box 2649
Columbus, OH 43216

World of Music by Jane Beethoven et al. A comprehensive music curriculum.

Rhythm and movement: Teachers' guides

The following texts are a small sample of the books about creative movement and rhythm. Each text contains a useful bibliography of other sources.

Braley, William T.; Konicki, Geraldine; and Leedy, Catherine. **Daily Sensorimotor Training Activities: A Handbook for Teachers and Parents of Pre-School Children.** Educational Activities, Inc., 1937 Grand Ave., Baldwin, NY 11510. 1968.

These sensorimotor activities are designed to be integrated with the curriculum and equipment used in early childhood centers. There are activities for developing awareness of body image, space and direction, balance, and basic body movements. Also included are activities for hearing discrimination, symmetrical perception, eye-hand and eye-foot coordination, form perception, and perceptual rhythmic activities for large and fine muscles. This is not a music text, but it is useful for rhythmic activities.

Cherry, Clare. **Creative Movement for the Developing Child: A Nursery Handbook for Non-Musicians.** Lear Siegler, Inc./Fearon Publishers, 19 Davis Dr., Belmont, CA 94002. 1971.

A book of rhythmic activities accompanied by chants or lyrics set to familiar nursery tunes. Beginning with "Crawling" activities, the program progresses through "Creeping," "Walking,"

"Running," "Leaping," to "Hand Movements," "Spontaneous Movement to Recorded Music," "Body Percussion," and "Auditory Perception Games." Prepared for teachers of children two and a half or three years old by a teacher who developed the activities while working in nursery schools.

Crews, Katherine. **Music and Perceptual-Motor Development.** Classroom Music Enrichment Units, the Center for Applied Research in Education, Inc., c/o Prentice-Hall, Inc., Englewood Cliffs, NJ 07632. 1975.

A handbook containing a variety of songs, musical games, and other activities that children have found enjoyable and teachers have found useful in helping children in their perceptual-motor development. The approach of the book is based on children's discovery and use of their bodies through games and music. The songs and musical games are arranged according to various concepts such as body image; laterality and directionality; basic shapes, sequencing; stress, duration, and tempo; and letters and numbers. Some songs are notated; for other activities, a well-known song or recording (and source) is suggested. A useful book for busy teachers.

Kenney, Maureen. **Circle Round the Zero: Play Chants and Singing Games of City Children.** Magnamusic-Baton, Inc., 10370 Page Industrial Blvd., St. Louis, MO 63132. 1974.

A collection of games and chants played "wherever children must make do with a sidewalk for play space." The text contains jumping rope chants, clap pattern songs, ball-bouncing games, counting out rhymes, call and response songs and chants, elimination games, and singing games. The author has preserved in this book a part of the exciting world going on in any neighborhood where city children gather on sidewalks and stoops to play together.

Nash, Grace C. **Verses and Movement for the Classroom.** Swartwout Productions, Scottsdale, AZ. 1976.

This book contains 75 action verses for classroom use, extending from group movement to tableau ideas. Good for needed changes of pace, release of energy, and development of self-direction and control. Some representative titles are "Walking in Space," "Punching Holes," and "Shadow Games."

Nelson, Esther L. **Dancing Games for Children of All Ages.** Sterling Publishing Co., Inc., 2 Park Ave., New York, NY 10016. 1978.

This collection contains more than 40 songs and games with piano accompaniment and instructions for games for children from three years old to those in upper elementary school grades. The author has included practical advice, tips, ideas, and inspirations that are useful to anyone working with young children. Many delightful songs and games.

Wax, Edith, and Roth, Sydell. **Mostly Movement Book 1: First Steps.** Most Movement Ltd., New York, NY. 1979.

This book contains stories and related musical activities for incorporating creative movement experiences in the curriculum based on the philosophy of Emile Jaques-Dalcroze. For children ages 3–8.

Weikart, Phyllis. **Movement in Steady Beat** and **Round the Clock.** High Scope Press/Research Foundation, 600 No. River St., Ypsilanti, MI 48197.

Rhymes, action songs, and games focusing on experiencing beat and movement to music. May be used to develop a movement curriculum. Accompanying cassette tapes.

Books about music in early childhood

The following books contain useful discussions about music in early childhood curricula and help teachers formulate realistic goals and objectives based on information about the learning and developmental characteristics of young children. One text (marked with an asterisk) includes songs, games, and materials for musical experiences in early childhood education; the others provide thoughtful insights about music and young children plus a limited number of sample music activities.

Aronoff, Frances W. **Music and Young Children.** Holt, Rinehart and Winston, 301 Commerce, Suite 3700, Fort Worth, TX 76102.

Andress, Barbara; Heimann, H. M.; Rinehart, A.; and Talbert, E. G. **Music in Early Childhood.** Music Educators National Conference, 1902 Association Dr., Reston, VA 22091. 1973.

Andress, Barbara, ed. **Promising Practices: Prekindergarten Music Education.** Music Educators National Conference, 1902 Association Drive, Reston, VA 22091. 1989.

Contains articles by well-known early childhood music educators who describe their programs in various ways. Some authors provide a comprehensive look at their overall programs; others describe specific song and rhythmic activities.

*Bayless, Kathleen M., and Ramsey, Marjorie E. **Music: A Way of Life for the Young Child.** C. F. Mosby Co., Publishers, 11830 Westline Industrial Dr., St. Louis, MO 63141. 1978.

Evans, David. **Sharing Sounds.** Longman Group Ltd., Churchill Livingstone, 23 Ravelston Terr., Edinburgh, Scotland EH4 3TL. 1978.

Described as "not about music, but a book about children," this book, by an English music educator, contains good discussions of the emergence of musical sensitivity in infancy—a more thorough discussion of this age than is generally found. Breezy, informal writing style; many songs, jingles, baby games, action rhymes, sound quizzes, and stories are interspersed throughout the text.

Feierabend, John, ed. **Tips: Music Activities in Early Childhood.** Music Educators National Conference, 1902 Association Drive, Reston, VA 22091. 1990.

Contains ideas for age-appropriate ways to introduce young children to music. Included are methods for developing musical concepts, managing groups of children, and developing community interest in preschool music programs.

Greenberg, Marvin. **Your Children Need Music.** Prentice-Hall, Englewood Cliffs, NJ. 1979.

Focuses on children's musical development from birth through age five. Information is provided about age-related musical development. Outlines specific methods for presenting lessons. Contains a song section.

McDonald, Dorothy, and Simons, Gene. **Musical Growth and Development: Birth Through Six.** Schirmer Books, A Division of Macmillan, Inc., 866 Third Avenue, New York, NY 10022. 1989.

This book describes the musical development of the young child from birth to age six, and provides guidelines for developing an age-appropriate music curriculum. Contains information about setting the environment, implementing the program, and accommodating children with special needs. Included is a song/suggested activities section for specific age groups.

Mulligan, Mary Ann. **Integrating Music with Other Studies.** Classroom Music Enrichment Units, The Center for Applied Research in Education, c/o Prentice-Hall, Inc., Englewood Cliffs, NJ 07632. 1975.

This text is a series of lesson plans that show how music can be integrated with other subject areas, and how musical experiences can be based on concepts similar to those in other subjects. The subject areas are social studies, science, mathematics, and language arts. Specific lessons for young children and elementary children are formulated in each subject area. Few songs are notated; rather, well-known songs and/or recordings are suggested for each lesson. Clearly written, easy to follow.

Recordings and cassettes

A great number and variety of recordings that are excellent for young children are available. Many come in both record and cassette form. Contemporary popular style, folk style, ethnic from different cultures, serious orchestral, band, and choral recordings—all should be included in a listening repertoire for young children. The following is a small representative sample of the available recordings.

For the very young

Loving and Learning from Birth to Three, by Diane Hartman Smith. #333. Joy Records, Box 58, Aspen, CO 81611.

Songs of love, security, and happiness: vocals with guitar, piano, harpsichord accompaniment. Some children's choruses.

Music for 1's and 2's by Tom Glazer (Songs and Games for Children #CMS649). CMS Records, Inc., 226 Washington St., Mount Vernon, NY 01553.

Music for the Morning of Life. Arrive Recording Studios, Box 3006, Ventura, CA 93003.

A collection of six records of orchestral, harpsichord, piano, and guitar music. Sudden dynamic changes have been modified. Classical music.

Songs to Grow On, by Woody Guthrie. Folkways Records, distributed by Roundup Records, P.O. Box 154, Cambridge, MA 02140.

For the very young child, songs composed and sung by folk artist Woody Guthrie. Guitar accompaniment. "Wake Up," "Clear-O," "Sleepy-Eyes," "Put Your Finger in the Air" are a few of the titles. Songs still loved by young children.

For ages three to six

Adventures in Music. RCA Records, Educational Sales, P.O. Box RCA 1000, Indianapolis, IN 46291.

A recorded library of traditional orchestral literature. The albums are classified according to grade level, but all the albums contain music of worth for all children. The albums developed for grade one contain short orchestral compositions that are very appropriate for use with younger children too.

Bowmar Orchestral Library (BOL). Bowmar, 4563 Colorado Blvd., Los Angeles, CA 90039.

Albums of standard orchestral literature. The album *Animals and Circus* includes Saint-Saëns's *Carnival of the Animals,* one of the selections used in the study by Turnipseed cited in Chapter 4. While all of the albums are recommended for use in early childhood education centers, a series for the very young listener has been developed entitled *The Small Musician.* Five recordings and a songbook constitute this series. The titles of these albums are
"The Small Singer," Record 1 #021
"The Small Singer," Record 2 #022
"The Small Listener" #393
"The Small Dancer" #391
"The Small Player" #392
(The Bowmar catalog, available upon request, lists many albums that teachers will find attract young listeners.)

The Elephant Tapes, by Sharon, Lois and Bram. Elephant Records; P.O. Box 101; Station Z, Toronto; Ontario, Canada M5N 2Z3.

These popular artists have produced a series of cassette tapes with accompanying instructor guides. The songs build language and rhythmic skills, help develop healthy social skills, and nourish fantasy. The series includes
"Elephant Show"
"Happy Birthday"
"In the Schoolyard"
"Mainly Mother Goose"
"Mother Goose Songbook"
"One Elephant, Deux Elephants"
"Singing 'n Swinging"
"Smorgasbord"
"Stay Tuned"

Golden Records. Educational Division, Michael Brent Publications, Inc., P.O. Box 1186, Port Chester, NY 10573.

Golden Records catalogs contain titles of many compositions

appropriate for use in early childhood. Among the many exemplary selections are

"A Child's Introduction to the Nutcracker Suite" (Tchaikovsky)

"Peter and the Wolf" (Prokofiev)

"Music of Great Composers"

The Hap Palmer Record Library for Young Children, by Hap Palmer. Educational Activities, Inc., 1937 Grand Ave., Baldwin, NY 11510.

These recordings feature contemporary "pop" sounds with vocals and guitar accompaniment. Representative albums include
"Learning Basic Skills Through Music"
    Records: AR 514, 522, 521, 526
    Cassettes: AC 514, 522, 521, 526
"Folk Song Carnival"
    Record: AR 524—Cassette: AC 524
"Feelin' Free"
    Record: AR 517—Cassette: AC 517
"Creative Movement and Rhythmic Exploration"
    Record: AR 533—Cassette: AC 533
"The Feel of Music"
    Record: AR 556—Cassette: AC 556
"Getting to Know Myself"
    Record: AR 543—Cassette: AC 543
(Complete catalog available upon request.)

Ella Jenkins Records. Folkways Records, distributed by Roundup Records, P.O. Box 154, Cambridge, MA 02140.

Ella Jenkins's folk, ethnic, and composed songs and activities are fine for use with young children. Some representative titles from her recordings are
"Nursery Rhymes—Rhyming and Remembering" R 7660
"Early Childhood Songs" R 7630
"Call-and-Response Rhythmic Group Singing" R 7628

To this list should be added recordings that are favorites of the children in your group and those that are your favorites. What is valued by the adults who are important in the lives of young children will be valued by those children.

Sources for ordering instruments

The following companies offer an assortment of rhythm and melody instruments. Brochures and catalogs are available upon request.

Childcraft Education Corporation, 10 Kilmer Rd., Edison, NJ 08817.

Rhythm and musical instruments; children's records of movement and rhythm, sing along, basic concepts, and poetry and story; and songbooks.

M. Hohner, Inc., Education Division, Andrews Rd., Hicksville, NY 11802.

Percussion instruments, Orff instruments, melodicas, pitch pipes, song flutes, kazoos, ukuleles, guitars, recorders, as well as many small keyboard instruments.

Peripole, P.O. Box 146, Browns Mills, NJ 08015.

Orff instruments, assorted other percussion instruments.

Rhythm Band, Inc., P.O. Box 126, Fort Worth, TX 76101.

Rhythm band sets and individual rhythm instruments, African, Native American, and Oriental instruments. Recorders, flutophones, tonettes, metronomes, autoharps, resonator bells, melody bells, step bells, handbells, school organs, pianos, guitars, and ukuleles are also available. In addition, film series (*Rhythms for Children*) and many music teaching aids including natural color photographs of the instruments of the orchestra and recordings may be ordered.

Index

Information about NAEYC

NAEYC is . . .

an organization of more than 103,000 members founded in 1926 and committed to fostering the growth and development of children from birth through age 8. Membership is open to all who share a desire to serve young children and act on behalf of the needs and rights of all children.

NAEYC provides . . .

educational services and resources to adults and programs working with and for children, including

• *Young Children, the* peer-reviewed journal for early childhood educators

• **Books, posters, brochures, position statements, and videos** to expand your knowledge and commitment and support your work with young children and families, including such topics as inclusion, diversity, literacy, guidance, assessment, developmentally appropriate practice, and teaching

• **An Annual Conference,** the largest education conference in North America, that brings people together from the United States and other countries to share their expertise and advocate on behalf of young children and families

• **Week of the Young Child** celebrations planned annually by NAEYC Affiliate Groups in communities across the country to call public attention to the critical significance of the child's early years

• **Insurance plans** for members and programs

• **Public policy information** and access to information through NAEYC resources and communication systems, for conducting knowledgeable advocacy efforts at all levels of government and through the media

• **A voluntary accreditation system** for high-quality programs for children through the National Academy of Early Childhood Programs

• **Professional development resources and programs,** including the annual National Institute for Early Childhood Professional Development, working to improve the quality and consistency of early childhood preparation and professional development opportunities

• **Young Children International** to promote international communication and information exchanges

For information about membership, publications, or other NAEYC services, visit NAEYC online at **www.naeyc.org**

National Association for the Education of Young Children
1509 16th Street, NW, Washington, DC 20036-1426
202-232-8777 or 800-424-2460